# Light My Candle

BY ANITA BRYANT

*Mine Eyes Have Seen the Glory*
*Amazing Grace*
*Bless This House*


BY ANITA BRYANT AND BOB GREEN

*Fishers of Men*
*Light My Candle*

# Light My Candle

**Anita Bryant** and **Bob Green**

Fleming H. Revell Company
Old Tappan, New Jersey

BV
4501.2
.B79

Library of Congress Cataloging in Publication Data

Bryant, Anita.
    Light my candle.

    1. Christian life—1960–   I. Green, Bob.
II. Title.
BV4501.2.B79       248'.4       74–19091
ISBN 0-8007-0690-0

84-678G

IN *loving memory of*

> Teddy Moody Heard
> Dan Topping
> Grandpa (John) Berry

# Contents

# Foreword

Literally millions of Americans knew Anita Bryant before her first book *Mine Eyes Have Seen the Glory* was published in 1970. They knew her from the Bob Hope tours, numerous telecasts and personal appearances, TV and radio commercials, the Orange Bowl Parade and, of course, from the old Don McNeil's "Breakfast Club." They knew her as an attractive (a runner-up in Atlantic City's famed Miss America Pageant) and talented performer. Now, after her first and subsequent books, still more men, women, and young people have come to know Anita Bryant as a dedicated Christian—one who shares her strong faith through witnessing. They have come to know her as a wife and mother, a woman with frailties much like less glamorous folk—but always seeking His Way. Many have come to know the Green family almost as well as their own neighbors—perhaps even better. They've shared the triumphs and trials of Bob and Anita and through this family have come closer to Jesus Christ.

We at Revell are proud to be a part of Anita Bryant's book ministry.

THE PUBLISHERS

# Light My Candle

# Bob

## 1
## Trials and Triumphs

The other day I thought about something Anita once wrote in an earlier book—how life seemed so perfect it actually scared her. Questions nagged at her:

What if God should take anything away? What if life changed too much? What if someone we loved were to die?

I didn't understand. "You're nutty," I told her. "Why can't you just be happy? Why not thank the Lord for blessing us? Why can't you just enjoy His gifts?"

That was three years ago, when our faith had only once been severely tested. As the Bible says, "Tribulation worketh patience" (Romans 5:3), but in those days we knew almost nothing about tribulation and even *less* about patience.

Today is different. We've had a superheavy year, and it's by no means over. Without the Lord, we never could have made it this far.

This household in recent months has known sickness and death of loved ones, deep grief and heartache, day-to-day stress, business problems, emotional trauma—you name it!

We meant this book—*Light My Candle*—to help Anita share principles she's learned about the Spirit-filled life. But so much has happened in both our lives—many great victories as well as frequent, faith-testing trials—that she asked me to tell my part of the story.

Before we begin, let's introduce the Bob Green clan from Villa Verde, Miami Beach, Florida.

Anita Bryant, my wife, is widely known as "the Florida orange-juice girl," because of television spots and personal appearances for the Florida Citrus Growers. She's perhaps equally well known as a Christian entertainer—singer, recording artist, and television star. As her personal business manager, I'm very proud of her.

But as her husband, friend, and prayer buddy, I know many other sides to Anita Bryant Green that she's possibly shy about revealing. These are the traits I especially love and admire.

For example, I know Anita as Mommie to our four kids —Bobby, eleven; Gloria Lynn, ten; and twins Billy and Barbara, now five and one-half. She's an excellent mother: patient, involved, warm and loving, yet strict, always ready for fun or ready to teach them. Most important of all, Anita lives her Christian faith before our children. She leads them by example.

Of course I especially love the Anita who witnesses for the Lord, both publicly and one-to-one. I'm thinking of the gal who works late into the night preparing to teach Sunday school (she teaches eleven-year-old girls)—phones a friend to pray with her—visits a sick, lonely old man and cleans his kitchen—helps with Vacation Bible School—manages a big house, one husband, four kids, a dog, two birds, a pond of goldfish, and a cat—and still finds time to write books.

Anita and I have been married for fourteen eventful years.

She became a born-again Christian at age eight, while I was led to the Lord the night before our wedding. After the babies came, we got serious about establishing a Christ-centered home and family life. This decision revolutionized our home.

You'll notice that very often Anita and I refer to the Northwest Baptist Church and its pastor, Brother Bill Chapman. We love that Bible-loving, soul-winning church, where our four kids and I were baptized, where Anita and I, with Bobby and Gloria, entered the fishermen ministry, where Anita visits and teaches, I serve as deacon, and teach nine-year-old boys.

Five years ago Anita wrote her autobiography—a book entitled *Mine Eyes Have Seen the Glory,* a simple testimony of her Christian faith. To our surprise, it became a best seller.

Three other books followed in rapid succession. *Amazing Grace* records the struggles and miracles within one unforgettable six-week period of our lives.

Next, Anita and I collaborated on *Bless This House,* a book about Christian marriage. And last year we wrote *Fishers of Men,* which explores the subject of witnessing for Christ.

As we begin writing *Light My Candle* Anita and I are struck by a curious realization. Many chapters in this present book take up stories begun in our earlier work, or reintroduce people our readers remember from one of the previous volumes.

For example, my battles to lose weight provoked a fairly humorous chapter in *Amazing Grace*—and I received a flood of sympathetic mail about dieting. Today, three books later, I can report that diet plus the grace of God has wrought a real transformation in the physical Bob Green. There'll be a chapter about *this* miracle, I promise!

More soberly, I think of a supremely gracious postscript to Anita's closing chapter in *Fishers of Men*—the very moving account of the day President Lyndon Baines Johnson was buried. Anita will remember that day forever. President Johnson had desired her to sing "Battle Hymn of the Republic" at his burial service. Luci Johnson Nugent, his younger daughter, had relayed his request to Anita.

It's difficult to sing, unaccompanied, at services for a president of the United States. It's even more difficult to sing at the funeral of someone you love. Anita never before had encountered that painful a challenge except for the death of her Grandma Berry.

Maybe this is the place to share a letter we later received from Luci Nugent. With touching warmth and simplicity, her words reveal the sort of strength and faith that has made our nation great.

Dearest Anita and Bob,

My father used to say there were two types of friends, the talkers and the doers. Those whose friendships he truly cherished were those who did not expound upon the impossibility of production, but delivered without complaint. You were surely two of his favorite "can do" friends. Regardless of the inconvenience, whenever he needed you and called, you always appeared like manna from heaven with the voice of an angel.

Thus we were so very grateful when in the middle of the night we called you and you readily replied affectionately to our request to fulfill his often expressed desire to have you sing "Mine Eyes Have Seen the Glory" at his funeral. It was so fitting for you to share with those he loved a hymn that rejuvenated his spirit in life and confirmed his fervent belief that a greater life awaited him with his God. He would have been proud of you and we were.

When I recall the magical moments I shared with Daddy, so many of them surround you. How often were we in need of special entertainment and dozens of supporters started searching only to be calmed by my father's voice "get the best —see if we can get Anita."

Then I remember how touched I was by your taking the time out of your whirlwind schedule to come to see me in the hospital. It was a special thrill for me that Daddy was there and could visit with you on the personal level you both enjoyed. I was very distressed not to be able to see your performance and urged my parents to attend if they could, because you had always come through for us. Mother wanted to, but was concerned that Daddy needed a nap and wasn't going to get one, so they would have to forfeit the pleasure of hearing you. Daddy resolved the problem by promptly going to sleep in my hospital room, and I was elated later to hear from Mother, Daddy, and Patrick, as well as my physician, that there wasn't a dry eye in the house after your resounding "Battle Hymn of the Republic."

I also want you to know I remember his invitation to come for a visit and bring your family. I know he would want me to renew that invitation in his absence. I don't know what Mother's schedule will bring—nor does she. But sometime this summer I hope you will bring the children and we can stay at Daddy's home on the lake if not the ranch, and visit the library, the birthplace, the boyhood home, and the LBJ state park—and have a family vacation. He wanted you to come for he loved you—and we want you to if you still can —for our love lives on.

I am a phenomenally fortunate young woman to have known twenty-five years with a devoted father who was an inspiration and a joy larger than life. My world has been very blessed by his love and guidance and by your friendship. To know that all his efforts made the difference in your life as they did in mine will ease the pain of facing tomorrow without him.

Devotedly,

LUCI

God uses devoted friends to help us "ease the pain of facing tomorrow."

We're coming to understand the importance of shared joy and shared grief, both very liberating experiences. For example, Anita got just as excited over the fantastic success of Marabel Morgan's book *Total Woman* as though it were her own. Marabel came up with a super best seller—one we so much believe in—and her joy was our joy as we praised God for the whole thing.

On another level, we shared real anxiety and inevitable grief as Charlotte Topping, our sister in Christ, nursed her husband Dan through his final illness. That story of true Christian devotion and sacrifice began in Anita's book *Amazing Grace*. Later in this book, however, we will write its triumphant finale.

And equally close to our hearts, there is *Light My Candle*. The title of this book, with many of its concepts, anecdotes and illustrations, came from Teddy Heard, the very gifted and Spirit-filled wife of Judge Wyatt H. Heard of the 190th District Court of Texas.

There's no way to measure the effects of a Christian life such as Teddy's—a free, fun-filled, supereffective life—on other lives around her.

If you read *Fishers of Men,* you know Teddy Heard as a giver. One of the most valuable chapters in that book came straight from Teddy.

*Light My Candle* in every way truly reflects so much of her very special, healing light. You'll meet Teddy often in the pages of this book, just as so often this past year I'd catch Anita gabbing with her long distance between Houston and Miami—each talking hard and fast about some exciting new insight the Lord had given, or some answer to prayer.

When you meet an exuberant, beautiful mother of four children who knows and loves the Lord, possesses great creative powers, enjoys a happy husband, a fantastic sense of humor and really abundant life—like our Teddy—you know you've discovered something rare.

As I said, for months she and Anita kept the long distance lines humming.

And then on March 4, 1974, something unthinkable happened. Teddy Heard—our irreplaceable Teddy—went to be with Jesus. She was thirty-nine, approaching the height of her Christian life. Her four children ranged in age from sixteen down to seven.

Our world abruptly darkened. Some of us questioned God. Shaken, we wondered about the power of prayer, the practice of faith. Never before had some of us encountered such a profoundly personal shock, such a deeply faith-testing experience. Why had this happened?

But if our candles flickered momentarily, they did stay lit. Teddy's thesis—that God will light a candle in your spirit that He will never quench—proved its divine value.

*Light My Candle,* therefore, is written to show you and others exactly what Teddy showed us—a clear, graphic, exciting way to understand and share God's plan of salvation and how to live the Spirit-filled life.

Jesus said, "These things I have spoken unto you, that in me ye might have peace. In the world ye shall have tribulation: but be of good cheer; I have overcome the world" (John 16:33).

Teddy knew how to have that peace.

She showed us how to let the Light of the World shine forth from our lives. Today she is part of that glory of eternity which she so desired not just for herself and her family, or for Anita and me, but for you also.

Praise the Lord!

# Anita

## 2
# Light My Candle

"Girls, let's just draw a little picture to illustrate how God wants to use our lives."

I can still hear Teddy Heard saying those words, her Texas drawl (which I loved to mimic) so soft and casual that you'd never suspect she was about to set off a charge of real spiritual dynamite!

It was August, 1972, at the Anita Bryant Summer Camp for Girls. Teddy's group of young charges crowded close to see what she would draw—a small circle, as it turned out, ringed by a somewhat larger one, with a third circle surrounding the others.

Teddy surveyed the curious little faces for a moment. Her dark brown eyes sparkled, dimples twinkled, as she watched them try to figure out what she meant *this* time.

"Man is a trinity," she explained, pointing to the three rings. "In the beginning God made our body. Then He gave us a living soul, including will, intellect and emotions.

"And in the center, the first circle which is the spirit." Quickly she sketched in a candle. "He breathes into us the breath of life," she said, "and that is *God's* Spirit breathed into us.

"Psalms 18:28 says, 'For thou wilt light my candle. The Lord, my God, will enlighten my darkness.' "

I pulled my chair closer and watched, fascinated, as Teddy illustrated her uniquely beautiful way of presenting the Gospel.

Her three circles literally were to revolutionize my methods of witness. I'm so grateful to Teddy for sharing this, for the kindergarten-simple drawing, with selected Scriptures, helped me lead many people to the Lord.

Now I want to pass it on to you (the whole idea, including diagram and Scripture passages) because right this minute you know at least one person who is hungry for salvation and the Spirit-filled life.

Anyone, you see, can grasp this concept instantly, thus visualizing what man is and how Jesus does come into us, and lights our candle. It really works! Teddy's "three circles" can lead anyone—college professor or preschool tot—to understand how God wants him to live. (My pet name for the three circles is "Teddy's trinity.")

First, let's study Teddy's diagram. It's easy to understand.

Surely we all know about the "God in three persons," but how many people realize that man is a trinity also? Read the first chapter of Genesis where God describes how He made a body from the dust of the earth, how He breathed into us the breath of life, and how He lit the candle of our *spirit.* And man became a living soul.

Man a trinity? Yes! We are created in the fullness of the glory of God!

What I like about these circles is that the initial lighting of the candle means salvation—being born again, joining the family of God. This is a matter of opening your heart to Him. (*See* Romans 10: 9–11.)

# TEDDY'S TRINITY

*Psalms 18:28 "For thou wilt light my candle:
the Lord my God will enlighten my darkness."*

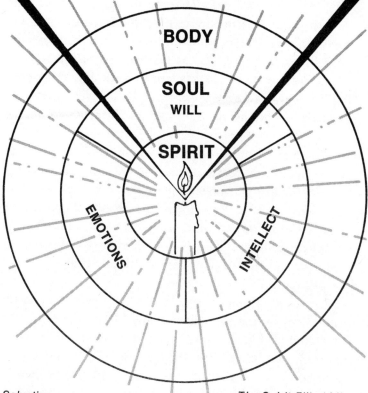

BODY

SOUL

WILL

SPIRIT

EMOTIONS

INTELLECT

*Salvation*

Genesis 1:26,27
Genesis 2:7-23
Isaiah 53:6
Romans 3:23
Romans 6:23
Hebrews 9:22
Psalms 18:28
John 1:1-14
John 3:1-19
Romans 10:9-13
Ephesians 2:8,9
1 Timothy 2:5
1 John 5:13

*The Spirit-Filled Life*

Philippians 4:13
2 Corinthians 3:17
1 Thessalonians 5:16-24
1 Corinthians 5:13
1 John 1:1-10
2 Corinthians 4:5-18
Psalm 119
Psalm 130
John 8:12
John 9:4,5
John 15:7-12
Luke 7
Proverbs 3:5,6
Proverbs 4:18
Ephesians 6:10-20

In Philippians 2:12, the Bible describes the working *out* of our salvation. (*See* 2:17.) That means that once your candle is lit by God the Holy Spirit, then through obedience, Jesus says, "If you love me you will follow my commandments" (*see* Matthew 19:17). *That* is the working *out* of salvation. What God works *in* He wants us to work *out.* The moment Christ comes in we are promised He will never leave us, and that we have eternal life right then and there. (*See* Ephesians 2:8,9.)

However, we must obediently follow His Commandments if the light in us is to shine out. As God shows us what to take out and what things to place into our lives, He allows that light in us to shine forth as a beacon, as we become released from first one dark area of life, then another.

What a marvelous picture—not just our salvation portrait, but also a picture of us walking with and being filled with God's Spirit!

Jesus said, "I am come that ye might have life, and that you might have it more abundantly" (*see* John 10:10). The abundant life requires a daily walk with Him, and I must be obedient to God to know the Spirit-filled life. Just because God lit my candle I can't suppose it will automatically shine out—that God will do everything for me.

Jesus paid for my sins on the cross, and if I look to Him by faith I will live. It's that simple. Even little children can come to Him. "Suffer little children, and forbid them not, to come unto me: for of such is the kingdom of heaven" (Matthew 19:14).

Teddy's trinity also illustrates—even beyond salvation—the important daily walk in the Spirit. No matter where a person may be with the Lord, this simple diagram can meet his needs.

And what about lost souls? Whether an individual is lost

from eternal life, lost from usefulness, or lost from fellowship, the three circles will speak to his condition.

Now, let's glance at the "Light My Candle" diagram. Maybe you'd like to show it to your children, as I did to our four-and-one-half-year-old Billy and Barbara. I simplified the story to suit their comprehension, and they loved it.

Youngsters enjoy drawing the circles. It's easy to trace around a salad plate, a saucer, and a juice glass to get three perfect spheres. Most of the time I just draw them free style.

The first thing to do is to explain the trinity of man, as God designed us: body, soul, and spirit. (Read Genesis 1:26,27; 2:7–23.) I then draw my candle in the center circle—but sketch it unlit.

With this beginning, you are ready to tailor your presentation for child or adult, Jew or Gentile. It speaks to anyone, whatever their spiritual condition, lost or saved. For the interested Jew, you may first use all Old Testament verses, then give the Plan of Salvation to explain the diagram. For Christians who want to grow, you share the Scripture verses concerning the Spirit-filled life! The illustration in this book provides some of my favorite Scripture references, but you may want to seek out others.

In brief, you're drawing a picture of salvation and of the Spirit-filled life—how we can walk in the Spirit and release the Spirit daily.

Even a child can see what being saved, or being born again, means. And as you sketch in the candle flame and convey the thrilling news that God Himself can light the candle, you begin to draw rays of light outward from the spirit, through the soul and past the body as represented by the circles. (Read the first chapter of John.)

I love the way Teddy explained the stages of God's light.

The first stage is *awareness* of God's light; the second is *acceptance;* and the third step is *release.* (*See* Matthew 5:16.) Thus the Spirit of God, operating through the fulfilled Christian life, sheds His light and life and energy into the world!

When I draw the three circles, I never seem to explain it exactly the same way twice. The Holy Spirit makes such beautiful and creative use of the whole thing!

Anyhow, I'll try to sketch in some typical ideas that might come out as we're drawing the circles, the candle, the flame, and the light rays.

Let's tell some of the Creation story in Genesis. Isn't that exciting?

In those days, God was a very personal God. He walked with Adam and Eve in the Garden. He talked to them. Let's say there was a candle in Adam's spirit and that not only was it lit, but shining out in all majesty and fullness of the glory of God.

God made man in His image. He made us glorious.

Adam had marvelous intelligence. For example, he could name every one of the animals in his world. Physically, his body was superb. He could take care of all the land watered by the four rivers within the Garden of Eden—an immense amount of land. When we contemplate Adam, we begin to get an idea of the potential the Lord God sees in us.

Jesus echoed that idea when He said we'd do even greater things than He had done. God gave us the potential to rise to very great heights.

As I sketch the candle, unlit, I tell how Adam was created perfect. From the beginning, God gave us a choice as to whether we would love and obey Him. As we lead our own children by love, rather than by force, so does God allow us to come to Him of our own loving free will.

God wanted Adam and Eve to choose the right way. Eve had only two Scriptures to memorize and she blew it. When the serpent misquoted God's Word, she believed the devil's lie and fell right into his trap. So Adam succumbed because of Eve's willful disobedience. God, being just and holy, had to punish them so He blew out their candles.

Yet, He still loved them. Even as they were banished from the Garden, He told them the seed of the woman shall bruise the heel of the serpent—and that was God's first promise of the coming Messiah. (*See* Genesis 3:15.)

So, being inheritors of Adam's sin, we must be born again. When someone is saved, from *what* is he saved? In Isaiah we learn, "All we like sheep have gone astray" (53:6). And in Romans, "All sin and fall short of the glory of God" (*see* 3:23).

The Bible tells how God required a blood sacrifice, for He said without the shedding of blood there is no remission of sins. (*See* Hebrews 9:22.) The Jews would use a perfect lamb, the most innocent creature, and it could not have one black hair on its body. Psalm 22 offers the most perfect picture of the Messiah, that He would take on the sins of the whole world.

That's why Jesus was called the Lamb of God (*see* John 1:29,36), because the bloodline comes through the male parent. God being Jesus' Father, instead of His having an earthly father, His blood was pure enough to cleanse the world of its sins. The beautiful thing is, that even as Adam and Eve sinned, God knew the propitiation for their sins and ours.

He said, "Let *us* make man . . ." (*see* Genesis 1:26). Jesus was with Him from the beginning. Thus the Holy Trinity—

Father, Son, and Holy Spirit—existed from the foundation of the world.

When you speak of being born again, speak of joining the family of God and that we need to receive Christ, and it's *God* the Holy Spirit who lights the candle.

When Adam and Eve sinned, God literally blew out their candles so that they no longer had immortality. They had a living soul, and a body, but they had no spirit.

Jesus said, "Behold, I stand at the door, and knock: if any man hear my voice, and open the door, I will come in to him" (Revelation 3:20).

But you of your own free will have to *open* that door. Then God Himself lights your candle. You allow Jesus to come, but *His fire* lights your candle.

How glorious! Too many Christians, however, consider that the final step. Now it's time to consult 2 Corinthians 5:12, Matthew 5:14–16, and 1 Thessalonians 5:16–24.

Many of us allow God to light our candle, then quench the Spirit and refuse to let Jesus really take over our lives (will, intellect, and emotions). Sometimes we make salvation seem easy for people, and then they don't grow.

God never promised us a life without tribulation. Life is rough for the believer as well as the nonbeliever. He does promise, however, that if you allow Him to—He will live your life with you and you will overcome trials.

God promises that once the candle is lit, He will not quench it. Only *we* can quench the power of the Holy Spirit (*see* 1 Thessalonians 5:19). God says *if* you keep His Commandments, His love and joy will remain with you.

Another promise says, "He that believeth on the Son hath everlasting life: and he that believeth not the Son shall not see life; but the wrath of God abideth on him" (John 3:36).

About a year ago, when Billy and Barbara were visiting me in my bed, I decided to show them Teddy's trinity. I thought they would enjoy it.

I started with Creation, as always, explaining it in child-like terms. I told about man sinning, and how God had to keep His word and send Adam and Eve from the Garden, which meant their candle was put out.

I explained that they had heard many times about how we must be born again, or saved, which means God wants to relight your candle. They knew about Jesus, how He died on the cross, rose on the third day, and saved us from our sins.

The twins seemed fascinated.

"Mommie, my candle's not lit!" Billy exclaimed.

"Mine is," Barbara said emphatically.

I recalled that many months earlier, at family devotions, Barbara told us she'd had some dreams about monsters. She prayed not to be scared of monsters anymore.

Suddenly she had to go to the bathroom, and Gloria took her. When they returned, Barbara said, "I'm not scared of monsters any more. Gloria told me to ask Jesus into my heart and I wouldn't be scared of monsters.

"I did, and I'm not scared anymore."

"Yes, Mommie, I led her to the Lord," Gloria said.

Then Barbara knelt at the altar and prayed, "Thank You, Jesus, for coming into my heart. I'm not scared of monsters anymore."

Later I told Marabel Morgan I wasn't sure it was the real thing, but Barbara sure acted as if it were. And from then on, she didn't seem scared of anything. On many occasions we had shared this Gospel with the children. Still, can a three-and-a-half-year-old girl understand salvation?

So a year later, Barbara was reminding Billy and me of that transaction. "My candle is lit," she informed us.

"Mine's not," Billy said.

"Would you like to go to the altar now and ask Jesus to come into your heart?" I asked.

"Yeah," he said, tersely. "I don't want my candle dark. I want my candle lit."

Before we went to the altar, I drew the three circles for them and explained that Jesus wants them to love and obey Him and their parents, to be baptized, and to go to Sunday school, read the Bible, pray with Him, and in those ways they can release His light in them. Billy got quite excited at that.

At the altar, Billy asked Jesus to come into his heart.

He took the picture of his candle to bed with him that night. As I tucked him in, he asked, "Mommie, can you really see my light?"

"I sure can!" I assured him.

Eventually Brother Bill came over to talk with the twins individually. He told me, "At their level, they understand exactly what they did. There's no doubt in my mind that they are saved."

Having satisfied himself that Billy and Barbara understood about salvation, and after they made their decision public in the church, he baptized them. They looked tiny beside the baptismal pool, but quite unafraid.

"Wow, that's deep enough to swim in," Billy commented, impressed. And when he was immersed, he kicked his feet a little.

Our twins chose to be baptized at age four-and-one-half. The ceremony took place August 4, 1973, at Northwest Baptist Church in North Miami.

# Anita

## 3
# Let the Sunshine In

"So many people have little dark rooms in their souls," Teddy said. "These rooms are buried deep—so deep within our will, intellect, or emotions that we keep them hidden even from ourselves."

I nodded, allowing my mind to slip uneasily past a couple of dark corners of my own. "What do we do about it?" I asked.

"When we allow the Spirit of God to shine in these dingy areas of our lives, He rolls up the shades and lets us see the cobwebs, filth, and bacteria that lurked there for years. Light heals these unhealthy places," she explained. "Jesus cleanses any diseased area of your life that you will yield to Him. There is a freedom there. You are no longer dark in that area of your life.

"But when we keep some pet sin unconfessed, when we won't let God shed light in that dark room, sin darkens us in that area. Only Jesus can give us life; otherwise we are dead.

"I believe that when we are able to release a sin or a dead spot, God allows new energy to flow into us there," she concluded.

Teddy Heard, more than any other person I ever knew, displayed the accepting, nonjudgmental, healing love of Jesus. Invariably people felt immediately drawn to her.

Teddy's kind of love—the love of Jesus—comes from God. Watching that vibrant and enthusiastic youthful Christian in action, often I'd imagine Jesus Himself, for I could visualize the kind of personal magnetism which persuaded others to leave everything and follow Him. Until I met Teddy, I really never saw too often that kind of love embodied in a human being.

Teddy possessed a rare ability to listen, empathize, and relate your experiences to her own. It was in this context that she explained to me how even born-again Christians have, in their lives, little dark rooms—and we hold the keys to these closets.

I had told her of some dark areas in my life.

"We must love Jesus enough to take the key and begin to open doors to Him," Teddy told me thoughtfully. "Where the Spirit of the Lord is, there is freedom," she stressed (*see* 2 Corinthians 3:17). Teddy helped Bob and me begin to understand these truths.

I see such radical changes in our lives. So many of our friends, too, are having to re-evaluate. Changes are taking place, many of them for the good. Suffering helps us appreciate what we have.

Take Charlotte Topping, for example. For many months Bob and I watched her minister to Dan, her husband, who for seven years suffered with disabling emphysema.

Three years ago Brother Bill and I helped lead Dan, Charlotte, and their five children to the Lord. Praise God for that! And always, from that day to this one, I felt dread and concern about Dan's state of health.

As he slowly declined, we saw less and less of Charlotte. Dan grew weaker by the day, drifting in and out of consciousness, and his weight dropped to 139 pounds. Not only did Charlotte faithfully attend her ill husband, but she had to be both father and mother to their youngsters.

It hurt to see the burdens she carried, the mental and emotional strain.

Meanwhile, our lives grew ever more hectic. Bookings were heavy; phones rang; mail flooded us. Tensions became part of every day. Bob began to overeat as compensation for some of the pressures he was under. He was becoming huge!

I began to worry about Bob. I knew he sometimes had spells of his heart beating too fast. That made him feel bad, and he'd have to lie down.

How do you get a stubborn man to a doctor? When at last he got so uncomfortable that he wanted to see a doctor, he didn't like what he heard. He needed to lose weight. His blood pressure was elevated. He'd get irritable over nothing and snap at the kids or me.

So the web tightened. As stress increases, as unhappiness grows, people tend to keep their troubles to themselves. I had a lot of things churning around in some dark basements of my life, but up on the ground floor, immediate pressures continued to mount.

Bob simply did not act like himself. He stayed tired, overweight, jumpy, and mean. He grew ever harder to live with. As for me, I began to experience a recurring dread that something bad would happen to my husband. Sometimes I feared he'd have a heart attack. Then I'd get mad that he was so concerned with himself, especially his body. Other times, I convinced myself he wanted to leave me. I could discover no reason whatever for this dread, but it kept returning. All of this was very, very real.

Depression crowded in on me with great regularity. I could not seem to control my emotions. Fear sometimes ran away with me, and no amount of rationalization helped.

I prayed about the fear and Teddy prayed with me. As we battled these frequent assaults of the devil, we prayed for new insights.

One day a friend phoned from another state to say she had been praying for me and the Lord seemed to give her a message. She felt led to telephone me, but the words seemed to make little or no sense. Nevertheless, she obeyed the Lord's leading.

"Anita, the Lord wants me to tell you that Bob is not your father, but is your husband. Does that make any sense to you at all?" She sounded perturbed. She had no way to know about the strains and tensions Bob and I were enduring or that fears concerning him had begun to invade my life.

"Not really," I said noncommittally. "Was that all? That's a funny message."

And so it seemed, until Teddy helped me interpret it.

"Anita, that's neat!" she said, very excitedly. "Isn't the Lord *good?*

"Think about it. You just had your thirteenth wedding anniversary. You didn't do anything special, and both of you felt exhausted and depressed. You know, I think you're returning psychologically to that point in your own parents' marriage. Do you realize that at just about thirteen years or so, they were divorced?"

Yes, but I still didn't get the significance.

"Anita, Bob is your husband, not your father. It was your mother who divorced your father. Bob, on the other hand, is not your father, but your *husband.* He loves you devotedly.

He's not about to die, and he doesn't want to leave you.

"See where those fears came from?" She sounded totally triumphant about an obvious psychological breakthrough. I began to see some light.

"Gee, Teddy, I see what you mean about allowing God to let some light into those dark rooms. Just because Bob hasn't acted very lovey-dovey lately, because he's irritable and snappish, I reacted from fear—a fear from far back in my childhood. It haunted me."

So I prayed about fear, and Teddy prayed with me.

"You know," she said at last," I think you need to go even deeper than that. I think there's another dark room the Holy Spirit wants to illuminate."

Her voice was very gentle. I knew exactly what Teddy referred to, but I could not immediately answer.

My father. For several months I'd carried a burden on my heart that I must see my father, must talk to him as one adult to another. I prayed for the Lord to send a special opportunity for this.

Sandra, my sister, had written that Dad was ill. He had a potentially dangerous-sounding condition that caused him to wear a neck brace, and Sandy seemed considerably concerned about him. Since he and I had had very little communication over the years, I hardly felt called upon to contact him now. Besides, there seemed to be nothing I could do for him.

Underneath, however, I experienced increasing amounts of anxiety and sorrow. "Is Daddy going to die?" I wondered. I thought how young he was, how strong and vigorous he'd always been, and felt great pain for him.

Still, I did nothing more than pray. As much as I wanted to write or telephone him, something kept me from doing it.

*(Let him get in touch with me. He knows where I live.)*

So pride kept me from reaching out to him, until pain began to plague me when I'd pray. One day the Holy Spirit stopped me cold, as urgent questions hit me broadside. Why are you concerned about your father's possible physical death? What about the death of his soul? Do you know if your dad is saved?

Meanwhile, I had slowly begun to own up to an ugly truth buried deep, deep within me. Bit by bit, I began to let myself see that I hated my father—hated him, though I pretended otherwise to the world and myself. I had put all the blame for the divorce entirely on my dad.

I had to give that hate up to the Lord. Teddy had been partially responsible for showing me this. Cautiously I began to let light shine into that darkest room of all.

This painful discovery was something I could not even admit to myself. In previous books I had written of my parents' divorce, and said I had forgiven my father.

The truth was, I had said the words—believing I meant them—but I realized now I still harbored hatred toward him.

God knows our hearts. My heart in all those years had not changed toward my father, not deep down. There was no real love in me for him, not the kind of love that God can give.

I had manufactured the word *forgiveness,* but there was no relationship built on that, and there was an empty space where a father-daughter relationship should be.

Also, the Lord began to show me that many of my tensions and resentments towards Bob stemmed from that unsatisfactory, unresolved relationship with my father.

Even after God gave me these insights, however, I still found no impetus and no heart to initiate any sort of healing. Things dragged on for long days and weeks. Then the postman delivered my answer in the form of a high-school graduation announcement from Sonny, my half-brother.

Warren Bryant, Jr., is some years younger than I, and my only brother. I have three stepsisters from Jewel's former marriage. Even though we didn't grow up together, I do feel considerable fondness toward him. I wanted to think of something really special for his graduation present.

Bob always has been an idea man, but this past year he has exhibited more and more of what I would call wisdom of the Lord.

"Why not phone Sonny and ask what he'd like for graduation?" Bob suggested. "Maybe he'd like to come here for a visit. And in any case, you could talk to your father."

I just stared at him. I had shared very little of the turmoil I felt concerning my father, but now I saw he perceived it anyhow. Bob knows me so well. He can read me like a book. Now he was offering me a way to do what I really wanted to do, but was too cowardly to face up to.

I placed the call. Sonny answered the phone. We chatted for a moment or two, when he did something completely disconcerting. "Hey, Dad!" he called. "Come talk to Anita!"

I literally broke out in a cold sweat. I felt paralyzed, totally unrehearsed and unprepared. I knew I needed to talk to my dad, but I was not ready. My mouth turned dry inside.

"Hi, Anita!" His voice sounded calm enough, but as we continued I could hear as much strain on his end of the line as on mine. To my horror, the conversation began to veer out of control. I would accuse him of neglect and indifference, and he would counter. We began to air our injuries and hurts, and very little understanding resulted.

Just when the whole thing grew intolerable, when I felt almost too dismayed and disappointed to bear it, Dad did something that jolted me apart.

"I love you, Shug," he said quietly, and then he stopped. He didn't say another word. The argument was over.

Emotions long suppressed instantly overwhelmed me. "I love you, too, Daddy," I choked out somehow, and then great sobs tore loose.

I seem to remember that we just wept together. At last, somewhat more composed, we agreed we would meet soon and talk. We would make honest, prayerful attempts to begin this failed relationship anew.

The conversation completed, I just walked into Bob's arms. He held me and comforted me in silence.

The tears flowed for hours, until I was exhausted with weeping. The healing that comes when God's light floods into long darkened rooms had begun its work in me.

# 4

# Crisis

"Always expect the unexpected," I tell Anita.

I'm no pessimist, but I *am* her personal business manager. Anita and I live in the high-pressure world of show business, where anything can happen at any time—and usually does.

You have to stay flexible, willing to alter plans, shift schedules, to make numerous decisions without blowing your cool.

I considered myself fairly good at the whole thing. For years I have guided Anita's contractual and travel arrangements, and now I head two other enterprises involving talent and personalities: Bob Green Productions, Inc., and Fishers of Men Opportunities, Inc. I see myself as someone who knows how to cope with the nitty-gritty.

So you chug along, never imagining anything could throw you, until—as the Bible says—time and chance change the whole picture.

For man also knoweth not his time: as the fishes that are taken in an evil net, and as the birds that are caught in the snare; so are the sons of men snared in an evil time, when it falleth suddenly upon them.

Ecclesiastes 9:12

My time came in July, 1973. Ironically, I'd just put together some beautiful plans for our family—an elaborate itinerary for the six of us, including business, fun, family reunions, and testifying for the Lord.

"Bob, I can't believe how many great things you crammed in this one trip," Anita marveled. "You worked everything out to the $n$th degree. The Lord sure must have helped you!"

I had to believe it. We had ten fantastic days ahead of us —time which included, among other important things, a chance for Anita to visit her father.

So tight was our schedule, however, that this once—despite traveling with all four kids—I had allowed no leeway for the unexpected.

We were only three days out of Miami Beach when our trip turned into a time of terrible fear. Our complicated plans went haywire.

And for once I really couldn't do much coping—because when the unexpected happened, it happened to *me*.

All systems were "go" on July 2 when the Green family arrived in Oklahoma City, Oklahoma, where we were to appear on NBC's "Stars and Stripes Show," hosted by Bob Hope. We felt quite excited to see Bob Hope again, and pleased to participate in NBC's Independence Day tribute to the USA. We enjoy doing patriotic shows.

We were especially proud that this show was originally started by Lee Allen Smith of WKY-TV (the station Anita started singing on at eight years of age), and was supported by the Oklahoma Broadcasters' Association.

This one paid tribute to America's returned prisoners of war—men like Howard Rutledge who only months earlier were incarcerated in Hanoi jails. We were excited to meet these heroes, plus others on the program—such personalities as Dick Anderson and Howard Twilley of the Miami Dolphins, Tennessee Ernie Ford, Bud Wilkerson, Mickey Mantle, and other favorites.

Anita had a long day of rehearsals, punctuated by sittings for Leonard McMurray, a sculptor commissioned to create a bust of her for the Oklahoma Hall of Fame, part of the Oklahoma Memorial Association.

The show that night turned into Old Home Week, as Anita's kinfolks started arriving from all over Oklahoma. Bobby and Gloria waited on pins and needles for Anita's mother and stepfather (Mr. and Mrs. George Cate) who were going to take our two oldest kids for a couple of days' visit. Bobby and Gloria were about to have their first separations from mommie and daddy, and, wow, did they look forward to it.

Anita comes from a big, close-knit family, and she doesn't get to see them any too often. As her kin people arrived, she grew progressively more excited—as keyed up as a little kid.

Sandra, her only sister, came with her husband, Sam Page. There were cousins—Virginia and Derrell Speers and family, and Patsy and Wendell Crittenden and family. Then, to her total joy, the Crittendens brought Grandpa Berry, the beautiful old blind gentleman who meant so much to Anita and Sandra when they were kids in Oklahoma.

Grandpa Berry's type of Christian believes in vigorous witnessing. He'd walk up to anybody and ask if they knew Jesus. That night he approached just about everybody on the show, witnessing to all the celebrities. "Yes, sir, I'm born again!" Tennessee Ernie Ford assured him.

A few weeks prior to our trip, Anita and her dad, Warren Bryant, had enjoyed a really special telephone conversation which was to help clarify some misunderstandings. I felt really grateful to God for that.

When we first got married, Anita's allegiance was about 95 percent to her mother and 5 percent to her father. I tried to explain to her this was only natural, because she had lived with her mother. For years I had urged Anita to communicate as adult to adult with her father.

As a result of her added strength in Christ, she began thinking rationally about this very emotional subject. Through prayer, she was letting the Holy Spirit deal with her. At times she'd weep about her father, saying he didn't love her, and I'd say that had to be nonsense.

I encouraged Anita to do her part in restoring that relationship. I knew her father as a great guy, no matter what may have happened in the past. I felt our children needed his fellowship, and also felt sure he needed our fellowship.

Besides that, we who preach Christ and all the virtues of our faith would be hypocrites if we are unable to forgive our fathers or mothers for things that happened long ago. Christ, and Christ alone, supplies the strength for mending broken relationships. I feel deeply for people who don't have Christ in their lives—people who have serious hang-ups of one kind or another.

At the "Stars and Stripes Show" that night Anita, already high with excitement over seeing so many of her loved ones at one time, told me her cup really was running over. Then came a total surprise—Warren Bryant, Anita's dad, with his wife, Jewel, and still more cousins!

Great! Anita anticipated seeing her father at his ranch later that week, but she had no idea he'd arrive to take in the show. Warren Bryant looked tired and much older than he had when last we saw him, several years earlier. He'd had a real bout with his neck problem (a possible result of an automobile accident and bad nerves) so he wore a neck brace. His face looked pale and weary, but he seemed eager to see Anita.

Anita looked almost shocked. Her eyes searched her father's face, took note of the uncomfortable-looking brace, his awkward walk, the concern in his expression.

If Warren Bryant looked tired, we learned later it was for good reason. He had traveled for hours by automobile—a painful, probably unwise trip. Now he was here, his hazel-brown eyes looking directly into Anita's in a proud, yet pleading way.

Anita rushed over and hugged him with all her strength. She clung to her dad the way Gloria and Barbara sometimes hang on to me.

"I felt shock and fear when I first saw Daddy," Anita later told me. "Then I felt tremendous compassion toward him. I could see Daddy also had suffered, not just Sandra and me. At that moment all the resentments and hurts from far back in the past just drained away. I was set free from the bondage of hating my father!"

Rehearsing and performing a network show makes for an exhausting day. Add to that the family reunions, the four kids out of their natural environments, and you can imagine how tired we all felt the next day.

Our vacation had begun on a very high note emotionally, and there was much more to come. Bobby and Gloria were ready to depart with Anita's mother and stepfather for an exciting visit "all by themselves."

So all eight of us, together with mountains of luggage, headed toward Tulsa for an overnight stay with Howard and Julie Twilley (who really love the Lord and enjoy teaching Sunday-school classes and sharing their faith. Howard, of course, plays pro football with the Miami Dolphins as a wide receiver and Julie teaches Marabel Morgan's Total Woman Course).

We had rented a motor home—a good idea with all that luggage—and the kids loved it. First, we stopped off at the Oklahoma Hall of Fame (Heritage House) to see Anita's official portrait which had been donated by our book publishers, Fleming H. Revell Company. Then we took off for Terlton, Oklahoma, to drop off Grandma Cate, Bobby, and Gloria. (Pawpaw Cate had gone home the night before to get back to work.) As we traveled toward the Cates' house, it got hot and I grew more and more nervous. I was trying to diet, but that kind of trip throws a diet out of the window. Then the heat, confusion, lack of sleep, trying to drive an unfamiliar vehicle along roads I didn't know—well, the whole thing made Anita describe me as "a bomb ready to explode."

By the time we reached the Twilleys' in Tulsa the day had turned into a scorcher. The next day was even worse and we played tennis in the hottest sun imaginable—until I had to stop. Howard, Julie, and Anita got quite concerned at my huffing and puffing, and the way my heart pounded, but I'd had these spells before. "Probably all that overweight," I told myself. "You can't carry those extra pounds around without paying for it."

I knew I'd be okay, and I insisted we play another set.

Julie Twilley was really sweet. She insisted on inviting a

bunch of Anita's kinfolks for barbecue that evening, and we were to watch the "Stars and Stripes Show" televised on NBC. So we had a big, old-fashioned celebration with all the folks: Anita's mother and stepfather; her sister Sandra and brother-in-law Sam and their three daughters, Kathy, Lisa and Michele; plus our four kids, and the baby, Michael Twilley. Everybody got a big charge out of watching ourselves on TV until (very soon after) I hit the sack.

Anita and Howard stayed up late, she sharing Teddy's circles with him and both of them sharing some of the exciting things Jesus has done in our families. I knew I needed sleep, however. I didn't look forward to our early departure the next day, or the hot drive to Hitchita, Oklahoma, where we were to spend the Fourth of July at Anita's Grandma and Grandpa Cate's house (Daddy George's parents)—a great place for a family reunion. The kids were very excited about it.

After that visit, we all had other great plans ahead of us. The George Cates were bringing Bobby and Gloria down to the great-grandparents Cates, then taking them back to Terlton for the rest of their vacation. We'd take the twins to Six Flags Over Texas. Anita and the rest of us would visit her dad's ranch for the first time—a very important stretch of time, I felt.

And then, our trip would culminate in something tremendous. We were to fly to Denver, Colorado, where Anita would testify to a very special audience. Colonel James Irwin, the U. S. astronaut who "retired" so as to devote the remainder of his years to full-time Christian service, had established an amazing retreat for all returned POWs and their families, plus families of men still officially listed as Missing In Action.

"America has wined and dined these men, has given them parades and vacation trips, new cars, new clothes, newspaper interviews, and everything else imaginable," Jim told us. "But nobody has given them what they *really* need—a renewed contact with Jesus Christ."

Consequently Jim, with his devoted staff at High Flight, the Christian organization he founded, put together a fantastic series of retreats for these heroes and their families. All summer long Jim and Mary Irwin, and the other High Flight staffers—with a number of Christian volunteers from outside —ministered to the sometimes-overwhelming spiritual and emotional needs of this very special group.

It was a tremendous ministry, a unique idea, and a costly one. Jim Irwin actually mortgaged his house to pay some of the air fares, and numerous other individuals and businesses dug deep also. As this is written, nearly a year later, Jim still whittles away at the enormous debt he incurred for the purpose of serving our POWs and the MIA families. Monetary response has been generous, but he's still thousands of dollars in debt.

Driving toward Hitchita last July 4, however, my head was full of thoughts about events to come—each one important—some momentous. I really felt thrilled that we'd get to share in Jim Irwin's efforts. Equally important in a personal way, I really was praying for Anita to get right with her father. Great things would come out of that, I felt sure.

It was the kind of hot early morning where the sun makes heat waves shimmer before your eyes. I had to concentrate on the car ahead (Sam and Sandra Page and their kids, whom we were following to Hitchita), and I wished like everything we could have slept a little longer instead of hitting the road so early. (Anita and I had gotten up early, before the Twilleys woke, and had loaded all those heavy bags into the motor home but had not stopped long enough to eat break-fast.) Now I was feeling bad—weak, and nauseated. I honked for Sam's attention, then pulled the camper off the side of the road.

"What's wrong, Bob? You're white as a sheet!" Anita looked quite alarmed.

"I don't feel good," I told her.

Sam and Sandra showed some concern. Anita wanted to take over the driving. I didn't feel like arguing with anybody but intended to drive.

"Guess I should have eaten breakfast," I said, but it didn't fool Anita. I was pale and sweating, and Anita watched me like a hawk.

"Do you have pain, Bob?"

"A little. Like yesterday. Not really pain, more like a heaviness," I admitted.

But I wouldn't let anyone else drive. We made it into Hitchita okay, where Daddy George Cate's mother and daddy, Mr. and Mrs. Paul Cate, lived. Daddy George's cous-ins Oletta and Lonnie Beathridge were also there. Everybody loved on one another. They had a kitchen full of roast beef, fried chicken, fresh green beans, black-eyed peas, home-grown tomatoes, and blackberry cobbler waiting for us.

Ordinarily I would have eaten my way through that menu in great style. By now, however, I couldn't stand the thought. The question was, how long could I fake it? I felt so terrible it scared me—weak, dizzy, sick, my heart pounding, and heavy sweat breaking out.

I heard the kids clatter across the porch and whoop across the yard, headed for the blackberry patch. My head was spinning. Anita's voice, quiet and alarmed, seemed to come from far away.

"Bob, go in the bedroom and lie down. Right now."

I obeyed. A little while later, stretched out across the bed, I didn't hear Anita, in another room, as she phoned a doctor. I was too concerned with the tightness in my chest, the sick and exhausted feeling that overwhelmed me, to care about much of anything else.

"Where is the hospital, Grandma?" I heard Anita ask. "The doctor says get him over there right away." Her voice sounded tight and strange.

"In Henrietta, honey," Mrs. Cate said. "We'll get him there. It's only fifteen minutes away."

"Help me," Anita said. "I can see he's seriously ill. . . ."

I knew it. Outside the pain, cold fear tightened itself around me.

Everything is going wrong, I thought. This is terrible. Anita has *got* to go to her father . . . and the POW retreat . . . and the kids. . . .

It's weird—that feeling of total helplessness. And the fear that rushed in was even worse than the pain that wouldn't go away. I tried to force myself to think what to do.

"Sam, Daddy George, *hurry!*" I heard Anita urge. "We've got to get Bob to the hospital right now.

"I'm afraid it's his heart."

# Anita

# 5
# Decisions

Bob was scared, I could tell.

I had never seen him like that. He insisted on sitting up during the short trip to the hospital, but his face was white as chalk, and his hands felt cold and clammy.

*Hurry, hurry,* I silently pleaded as Sam Page, my brother-in-law, sped us to the hospital in little Henrietta, Oklahoma. To my surprise, the hospital had computer diagnosis facilities whereby the doctor could check Bob's heart with specialists in Tulsa. This relieved my fears considerably.

The doctor's preliminary examination reassured us even more. "Can't find too much wrong," he said. "Probably it's indigestion, what with travel, irregular meals, and so on."

I grabbed at that answer, wanting to believe it. But when he made an electrocardiogram and relayed it to Tulsa, we got a different read-out—a definite irregularity in the test.

The doctor advised us to head for Tulsa and admit Bob to the hospital for further tests the next day. His words felt unreal. Panic began to rise in me, and I resisted what I was hearing.

"Why, doctor? What's wrong? I thought you said indigestion. . ."

49

Patiently the doctor repeated the facts. It might be due to faulty equipment, but a definite irregularity showed up in Bob's electrocardiogram. He might be sitting on top of a heart attack. We'd better take no chances but get him to the hospital with all speed.

"But . . . but . . .," I protested stupidly, my mind whirling in all directions. We were supposed to be heading for Dad's house, but now we had to return to Tulsa for the night. Is this absolutely necessary? I wanted what was best for Bob but, strangely enough, I began to feel angry about the way our vacation plans were being disrupted.

Bob, meanwhile, was feeling worse. They had given him a sedative, and now the doctor advised our making the forty-five minute trip to Tulsa in an ambulance.

I began making decisions a mile a minute. Bob always does all that, and this was the first time in my life I had been in charge of an emergency situation.

Sam rushed me back to Grandma's house, where I tried to handle things as intelligently as possible. What to do with the kids? The motor home? What to tell Dad? What would Bob need in the hospital? Would someone help pack a bag for me?

We had to break up the party. The day had begun with such great expectations, but now the whole thing had blown apart—and *maybe* all because of faulty equipment, I thought. I would not let myself look at any other possibility.

But I had to make decisions quickly: I asked Daddy George to drive the motor home back to Tulsa with Kathy Page, Mother, and the twins. (We agreed to meet at Covey Page's house there.) Sandra drove Mother and Daddy George's car with Bobby, Gloria, Lisa, and Michele. They would leave the twins and the motor home with Sam's parents. Sandra, Sam, and family would look after Barbara and Billy. Mother and Daddy George were to take Bobby and Gloria back to their Terlton home as planned. Sam would drive me to the hospital in Henrietta, then follow us in the ambulance to Tulsa's St. Francis Hospital.

Fortunately I had sense enough to take along my Bible and my book of daily devotions (*My Utmost for His Highest* by Oswald Chambers) for the long ambulance ride.

Bob, sedated, was supposed to sleep. I rode along beside him, believing the whole thing was one big mistake. *We are supposed to go to Dad's. Instead, we're headed to a hospital to check out faulty equipment,* I told myself over and over.

Then I began praising the Lord and believing Romans 8:28: "... all things work together for good to them that love God, to them who are called according to his purpose."

Bob lay there with his eyes closed, but he took my hand and asked me to read from the Bible. For some reason, first I chose to read from my book of devotions—and I couldn't believe the message God had for us. "Fret not thyself, it tendeth only to evil doing," I read. (*See* Psalms 37:8.) Eagerly I devoured the rest of it: "Resting in the Lord does not depend on external circumstances at all, but on your relationship to God Himself." ... "Fretting is wicked if you are a child of God." ... "All our fret and worry is caused by calculating without Jesus."

Had God ever spoken to us more directly than through this small book, during those nightmarish moments? It was with a sense of profound relief that I turned to the Bible and began to read Psalm 100 and Psalm 101. How triumphant! How marvelous is our all-merciful God!

Reading those magnificent Psalms, my courage strengthened and my voice steadied. Even when Bob began to weep,

I felt a sure new control of myself. Although I knew he was worried, and for the first time I began to admit there might be reason to fear, simultaneously the Lord gave me the gift of self-control.

"Anita, I'm so sorry," Bob said over and over, in the hospital. He wanted me to go to Dad. They put him in the Intensive Care Unit and began to monitor his heart. The next day he would undergo a treadmill test, and if that checked out okay, he'd be released.

"Don't worry," I assured him. "It's all pretty routine, the doctor says. They'll let you out tomorrow. The Lord has His timetable for everything, and I guess He gave us a little delay." I took Bob's hand and began to pray God would give him a restful, anxiety-free night.

I spent the night with my sister and brother-in-law at his parents', Covey and Marguerite Page. The next morning I didn't hurry to the hospital, but took care of returning the motor home, assembling the children, and so on. When all was in order, I phoned Bob to ask when he'd be checking out.

"I'm not," he said. "The doctor wants to talk to you."

Fear flooded over me. Sam took me to the hospital and wanted to wait in the lobby for me, but Bob insisted that he stay in the room. My brother-in-law had become my stabilizing force, constantly calming and reassuring me. Instinctively, I knew to lean on him.

"Everything checked out fine, except the treadmill test," the doctor reported. "There's something wrong in there. I want to go in and probe with a catheter—find out the problem.

"Bob may be sitting on top of a heart attack. A heart catheterization involves some risk—there's a small fatality rate—but it's worth that risk if he's about to have a coronary."

Incredible—the matter-of-fact way he said those words, the calmness with which Bob and I heard them. Inside myself I wanted to scream. Outside, I sounded reasonably sensible as I attempted to respond to the terrifying facts.

The test is not simple. . . . The very act of probing could precipitate a heart attack that might be fatal. . . . If a coronary develops during the procedure, a nine-man surgical team could operate immediately. . . . There's a 30 percent chance there's nothing seriously wrong. . . . There's a possibility Bob could. . . . *Oh, no, I can't even think it!*

It really didn't sink in. I kept assuring the doctor that Bob would be fine. Bob looked so terribly upset, and the doctor kept reiterating the facts, but I didn't accept any of it, really —not then.

Somehow, God kept me calm and cheerful for a space of time. I prayed with Bob. I told him that the night before I had telephoned Teddy Heard, and she gave me a Psalm to read—Psalm 118—which she called "God's insurance policy."

As I urged him to read this Psalm, as he begged me to telephone various people to request their prayers, the icy fear that began somewhere around the edges of my heart moved inwards, faster and faster, until I knew I must rush from the room. I had to leave to make the telephone calls. But more than that, I could keep wearing that cheerful face only just so long.

It's strange how bad news seems like a dream. You walk through the hospital corridor automatically, looking perfectly normal, your legs carrying you forward as steadily as always, your mind marveling at how ordinary and complacent everybody else looks—when *your* world is shaken to its foundations.

Quietly and calmly, Sam and I walked to the exit just as

though everything were fine, in my mind knowing everything *would* be fine, that this was just a very bad dream.

Then, walking down the hospital steps, the unwelcome idea hit me—my first realization of what life would be without Bob.

It felt overwhelmingly painful. It almost paralyzed me. I pushed the fear away, unable to tolerate the thought for more than the merest second. My throat constricted and my knees buckled. Indescribable fear filled my chest.

"Lord, I give this to You," I managed to whisper.

Then, *at that precise moment,* He gave me a miracle.

Sam glanced down at his feet and there, inexplicably, he found a rusty fishhook. Does that make any sense? A fishhook on the ground outside the hospital?

"Isn't that just like the Lord, to have a little sign lying there for us!" I cried, amazed. I thought of all the fishhooks I had given Bob in the past—the expensive gold ring, the key chain, the lapel pin. Matthew 4:19 means something so special to Bob and me, and fishhooks, for us, symbolize that verse.

Not one of the custom-designed ornaments could mean to me what that rusty hook symbolized. I took it in my hands almost reverently, turning it over and over as I stood and marveled at God's very personal and specific comfort.

When I gave the hook to Bob, he cried. He taped it inside the cover of his Bible, and it remains there today.

Who shall separate us from the love of Christ?

That beautiful passage of Scripture—Romans 8:35–39—describes the boundless comfort of God we were to receive in the hours to come. Read those verses if you ever walk on the rim of raw panic. They will steady you and sustain you.

Thank God for Christian brothers and sisters! Now I turned to the telephone, as Bob had requested, and sought help from our loved ones. Charlie and Marabel Morgan were on vacation and couldn't be reached. Our pastor, Brother Bill Chapman, and his wife, Peggy, likewise were unavailable.

Frantically I kept dialing, silently praying to find those who would surround Bob and me with their prayers. Never before had I felt so needy, so afraid.

Teddy and Wyatt Heard—praise God!—were at home. Teddy ministered to me, prayed with me on the phone, loved me. Then she and Wyatt watched and prayed all night in Bob's behalf.

As I continued to telephone friends, my mind replayed events of the day: Julie and Howard Twilley had come to be with Bob, and had prayed with him. . . . I had asked God for His own strength, knowing that if I broke down Bob couldn't make it as easily. I prayed for courage and a stout heart, no matter what, and He supplied. . . . Throughout it all, Bob was terribly concerned about changing my plans to see my dad. I had to keep telling him it was in God's hands. . . .

Teddy. After she helped me I could say, "I know he is in God's hands and is all right." I was so strong, after that, that I knew it was the Lord, and not me.

I thanked God for my family—so sweet, so good, so willing to do anything and everything. Bob insisted that Bobby and Gloria stay with Mother and Daddy George, that they keep their vacation plans as normal as possible.

I asked them to prepare the children, lest something happen to Bob. And that evening, I gathered the twins close and prayed with them, and they each prayed for their daddy. I told them he was very sick and might go to be with Jesus.

The twins. Their prayers were so sweet. But can children their age understand what I told them? I had no idea, but it seemed best to prepare them to some extent. Bob and I believe in keeping our children in touch with all of life's realities. We want them to understand where their strength lies when life-and-death struggles occur.

It was late when I finally got to bed. I had to rise at five the next morning. I spent all the time and pains in the world with my hair and makeup, and chose a pretty yellow dress. When I walked into the hospital at six A.M. I was very brisk and all smiles—on the outside, at least!

"I know what you're doing," Bob said, grumpily. "You spent all morning fixing yourself up to come in here all perky and cheer me up."

"I wouldn't do that," I told him.

"You wore your brightest, sunniest dress so you'd look cheerful this morning," he continued, accusingly. I can't put anything over on him. He knows me so well.

I tried to act casual as attendants gave him injections prior to X rays and tests. Thoughts of the procedure ahead, the needle entering his groin, a long catheter snaking along his blood vessels, traveling incredibly tortuous lengths, finally entering the heart muscle itself—I had to force my mind away.

Before Bob entered the operating room he handed me a letter. His hand felt ice-cold as he gave me a long, thick envelope I didn't want to accept. Instinctively, I knew he wrote it in case he didn't come out of that room. I wanted to drop it on the floor, to refuse it, but of course I didn't.

Later, in the waiting room, I made myself read Bob's message.

Thursday, July 5th '73
10:30 P.M.

My dearest Anita—

The sweetest thing just happened. The orderly came in to prep me for tomorrow morning. He saw my opened Bible and started telling me how important the Lord is in his life. He didn't know who I was. He gave me a beautiful testimony while he was working on me and I would have done the same but I was too emotional.

After he was finished he asked if I'd like to pray with him. I said yes and he took my hand and prayed for me. At that point, I was crying but I still praised the Lord for what I was going through. In time of need, the Lord provided this stranger out of the blue to comfort me!

I praise the Lord for the best wife a man could have. We've had such a glorious life together. We are so blessed. You and the children have brought me such complete joy. I know I haven't shown it—forgive me for that—but deep down, my joy is complete. You are truly an angel of the Lord, Anita. I love you so much.

Your devoted husband,
BOB

P. S. Thank you for such a sweet moment in the ambulance. I know you'll be happy to know that I made a commitment to rededicate my life to the Lord.

Then Bob gave me the orderly's name and asked me to sign some books for him.

I read the letter, and read it again, and I cried. Gradually God restored peace to my heart, and I noticed a family in that room—people related to an elderly man who was critically ill.

Now I shared with them Romans 8:28 and Proverbs 3:5.

It helped to enunciate my faith. I began to draw Teddy's trinity for them.

The door burst open and in walked Daddy George. He had taken the day off work to come comfort me. I was so touched that he did that. Then Sam and Sandra came in, and laughed a little to see me with my open Bible, sharing the Scriptures with my new friends.

Soon the doctor appeared. When I saw his broad smile, my heart leaped up uncontrollably.

Everything was fine! The heart catheterization proved conclusively that Bob's heart was perfect! It was over! I started grinning from ear to ear, absolutely dazed with happiness and relief.

I rushed to Bob's side as they were wheeling him to his room and grabbed his hand.

"Praise the Lord!" I cried with real fervor.

Tears streamed down Bob's cheeks.

"That's all I did the whole time," he choked. "I was so scared . . . for you and the kids . . . so helpless . . . all I could do was praise the Lord!"

It felt wonderful to arrange for Bob's release from the hospital, even if business details were almost completely foreign to me. As a sheltered and protected wife, I literally had almost no experience in arranging for family needs prior to the past forty-eight hours.

Now I had to do what Bob ordinarily would do—handle insurance, check him out of the hospital, phone home for information. Bob was gaining a whole new view of me, I realized. How often had he told me I'd never be able to function on my own?

He was seeing that I could, and he complimented me on my common sense. It was good new knowledge for each of us to possess. I *could* make decisions, could get things done, if the need arose. With the Lord's help, of course.

And now Bob had another important thing to learn—how much my family and his friends love him. When Bob came down to the waiting room, he was amazed at his reception committee. Mom's baby sister, Betty, and her husband, Bobby Callen, and their kids, Rodney and Cindy, were there —they'd all been so helpful and kind. My sister, Sandra, and her husband, Sam, and their three daughters, Kathy, Lisa, and Michele were on hand. They had changed all their vacation plans to help us in any way they could. Sam's parents, Covey and Marguerite Page, who had literally given over their home and were so sweet and kind, came to the hospital. Mom and Daddy George, who were there when we needed them and gave us such support and comfort, had arrived with our kids. When Bob saw the clan assembled tears came again.

All that morning (and the day before) the phone calls were arriving. Brother Bill phoned, his voice quivering. Did we want him to fly up there? Doctor Bill Rittenhouse of High Flight had phoned the hospital earlier, and was informed that doctors expected Bob to suffer a heart attack. Bill had organized prayers for Bob. Bruce Howe phoned, offering to fly in, but I told him all was well. (He is one of Bob's closest friends.)

Before the crisis I had phoned Bob's parents but made light of the whole thing for fear Farfar (Bob's father) might not be strong enough (he was just recuperating from surgery). They had perceived how serious it was, though, and were joyous at the good news when I called back.

And so it went, one loving message after another to inform us of God's love. Our hearts were full to overflowing.

After we prayed and gave thanks, there was one other thing for Bob and me to do. The doctor had given him a clean bill of health.

What should we do now? Go home? Continue our vacation?

Bob said continue our vacation, proceed to Dad's, to Six Flags Over Texas, and on to Denver.

Continue? Would that really be wise? The doctor had given his okay and I suddenly realized that decision really belonged to Bob, not me. We would go ahead with our plans, as he wished.

Praise the Lord!

# Anita

# 6

# My Father's House

I praised God all the way to my father's house.

So did Bob, I'm certain, as I drove the two-and-one-half-hour trip to Dad's ranch outside Sasakwa, Oklahoma. Bob and I and the twins eagerly anticipated our first glimpse of Grandpa and Granny Bryant's several-hundred-acre spread, the Black Jewel Ranch. We yearned for the peace and quiet of those beautiful acres—a perfect spot for Bob's first hours of recuperation.

"Bob, I'm flabbergasted. We're actually on our way again!"

He smiled. "How do you feel?"

"Great!"

It was true. I felt too tired and too grateful to get all tense about seeing Daddy again after all these years.

How was it?

Just very sweet. Daddy held me tight. He and Jewel had been praying for Bob, and it was like God used our crisis to make my dad's heart go out to me and bring us even closer together. I felt a rush of real love towards my father.

As the day wore on, we relaxed and became very comfortable with one another. I even accepted the idea that Bob really was okay! And as we shared how God had supplied all our needs that week, it became a testimony to those in my father's household.

"It seemed like the worst thing that could happen, in the worst place, and at the worst time," Bob declared. "And yet —we truly can praise God in all things. We don't know why this episode happened, but we can thank Him, knowing He'll use the whole thing to our good."

Daddy looked thoughtful. Tired as I was—bone-tired, in fact—I wanted to share with him in private. Fatigue said, *Why not turn in early and get a good night's sleep?* My body felt desperate for sleep.

Nevertheless, after dinner the Lord urged me to find Daddy and speak to him quietly. Tomorrow might be too late. The house would fill up with relatives; there might not be another quiet moment.

I'm so glad I sought him out. My tiredness didn't matter at all. When Dad and I opened up, it was amazing how many things we discussed in our brief visit.

"Dad, God has been so good to us," I began. I told him about sharing my testimony that morning with the people in the hospital waiting room.

"A year ago I couldn't have done that," I told him.

I found a piece of paper so I could show him Teddy's trinity. I think I shared every verse of Scripture I'd ever learned. And when I got to talking about the Trinity, I shared how God had showed me that Dad and I had a barrier between us all those years, because I hated him.

"Now I can tell you I love you," I told him. "I don't want to talk about the past. I accept you today because I really love you."

Daddy really listened to me. I felt his desire to know me
—really know me—just as I ached to be restored to my
proper place in his heart as his daughter.

"Where the Spirit of the Lord is, there is perfect freedom,"
I said. "He has given me freedom. Never before in my life
would I have had the courage to say these things to you.

"Daddy, I've got to ask you something terribly important.
I really want to know—when I die and go to heaven—will
you be there?"

Daddy seemed completely flabbergasted by the turn our
conversation had taken. It was hard for him to answer me,
but I, having gone this far, refused to stop now.

"Daddy, will we share this father-daughter relationship
eternally? I need to know."

The silence lengthened until I felt a tinge of fear.

"You'll never know the agony I have lived with all these
years," he began slowly. "I sure haven't lived for the Lord
recently."

I asked if there were a time and a place where he gave his
life to the Lord.

"I think I'm saved," he said.

"Daddy, don't think that. *Know* you are saved."

"Yes, there was a time . . . long ago . . . but real at that
time."

"Daddy, that's all I wanted to know. Could you pray with
me now, and rededicate your life to Christ again?"

Unaccustomed to this type of conversation, I could see
Daddy felt too embarrassed to go further.

"I'll get right with the Lord," he promised.

"Daddy, this past week with Bob has convinced me there's
no guarantee any of us will live to see tomorrow," I said. I
literally begged Daddy to get right with the Lord right then

and there, but his pride wouldn't let him do it.

Suddenly I wanted to touch him. I yearned to reach out to him, to express my love. Timidly I placed my hand on his shoulder.

"Dad, I want to pray for you, to ask God to help you return to Him and to heal your neck."

I began to pray, praising God for the week's circumstances, and then the tears came.

"Lord, I know my dad is a proud man," I prayed. "I know *my* pride.

"Lord, strip him of his pride. I love him and You love him, and I will be so proud of him when he humbles himself before You, for he has been out of fellowship with You." I prayed so deep, so hard, and I was crying the whole time. I could hear Dad quietly crying, too.

I put my arms around him. "Daddy, I love you."

"I love you, Shug," he said.

Those were precious moments. That night sleep came early, but first I prayed great prayers of thanksgiving. Also, for some reason I felt led to add a strange request: "Lord, when we go to church tomorrow, if You want me to speak or to sing, send someone to ask me. If someone asks, I will testify."

The next morning we all trooped into the tiniest little country church you ever saw. The church was filled with Dad and Jewel's neighbors. My father ordinarily didn't go to church, though Jewel and Sonny did. Both of them had dedicated their lives to Christ a year before, and all that time quietly had prayed that Daddy would come back to Jesus. As I seated myself next to my father, the song leader immediately asked me if I'd share a song and a word of testimony.

"Praise the Lord!" I said, my prayer answered.

The Holy Spirit gave me my testimony. I thanked the little

congregation for their prayers for Bob. "God in His mercy spared Bob, and we are humbly grateful," I told them.

"Also, I want to publicly thank my father, for it was his testimony that he demonstrated before me at the time I needed it most—because when I was a child my father and mother taught Sunday school and were Christian examples before me—that caused me at age eight, by faith, to ask Jesus into my heart.

"I truly believe at that time of my life it was partly the example of my Christian father and mother that led me to my salvation."

Then I sang "It Took a Miracle" and "Amazing Grace."

A visiting preacher delivered the sermon that morning, and he really preached the Word. What a sermon! Our hearts overflowed as we worshiped together.

And when invitation time came, my father stepped out, went forward, and got on his knees! Instantly Jewel joined Daddy at the altar as he rededicated his life to Christ. As for me, the rain cloud simply burst open. I placed my head down on the back of the pew before me and wept. I sobbed unashamedly before all Dad's neighbors, and Bob cried, too.

Afterwards I went up and hugged my father.

"Daddy, I've never been more proud of you," I said.

And then I saw something wonderful. God had taken all the tension and tiredness out of Dad's face, the weariness and pain. Despite the neck brace, he looked like my same handsome daddy—and his face radiated peace and joy.

*Thank You, God. You are healing him,* I thought. My heart nearly burst with gratitude.

All afternoon, Dad's relatives arrived at the ranch. It was the talkingest, laughingest, praisingest time you ever saw. It was as though the doors had swung wide open for Daddy and me, and I could talk to him about anything at all concerning the Lord. There was so much to say, and so little time. . . .

The day wore on. It was a happy day, noisy with laughter and fellowship. The place overflowed with Bryant kinfolks. All afternoon I shared important things—Teddy's trinity, Dad's experience, Bob's deliverance—and we all rejoiced.

Suddenly, the Lord spoke to me very clearly.

"We're all going to church tonight," I told them. "That way we can have more fellowship and visit some more."

They all started giving excuses. Nobody was dressed for going to church. Some were barefooted, some in jeans. They just looked at me like I had lost my mind.

"The love of God transcends all barriers," I insisted. "Let's go worship Him."

"We can't go to church in slacks," the women said.

"Isn't it better to go to church dressed in slacks and worship with a happy heart, than not to go at all?"

So we all went, just that spontaneously. We must have filled three or four pews, and an odd-looking bunch we were. Again they asked me to sing and to share, so that gave me my chance.

"It's so good to know the love of God," I began. "My relatives felt funny about coming to church tonight, because they are not dressed for the occasion.

"I told them if you judge them as to how they look on the outside, your relationship to God is wrong to begin with. I'm sure you have the love of God in your hearts and won't point a finger at anybody.

"The love of Christ transcends all barriers. God looks on our hearts, not our clothing."

"A-a-a-a-a-men!" the congregation replied, as in one great voice.

Never have I felt more complete Christian accord within one body. As I began to sing "How Great Thou Art," something welled up in my eyes, and the bare feet and slacks and faces sweet with worship all blurred into an indescribably beautiful scene.

After church we visited some more and belatedly celebrated Fourth of July with fireworks we never got to use on the official Fourth. But this made it a trinity celebration: our country's birthday, Bob's restored health, Dad's rededication.

Never will I forget that time. My God, gracious beyond imagining, in two days' time had restored Bob to our household and me—with my family—to my father.

All along, I realized, Bob felt such an urgency for this to happen. And now it was done. I was happy beyond my wildest dreams. Bob rejoiced with me. Daddy and Jewel and Sonny were a family united in Christ.

God is so good!

I think of the beautiful Psalm 37, and especially verse 4: "Delight thyself also in the Lord; and he shall give thee the desires of thine heart."

This He has done for me, I know. I am beginning to realize, however, that *first* I must delight myself in Him. All else will follow.

# 7

# High Flight

There are times in any life where, looking back, you clearly see how you took a wrong turn.

The weeks after my heart catheterization became just such a turning place for Anita and me. We had sustained a severe shock. This brought us to a supercloseness and dependence on the Lord beyond anything either of us had ever known.

We emerged from our trauma extremely tired physically, but exuberant in mind and spirit.

"Praise the Lord, the worst time of our lives is over!" we said. We reasoned that He had some great lesson for us in the whole thing.

This is true, but the experience was *not* over. In fact, it hardly had begun. The strains Anita and I were to endure in the months ahead tested us—and our marriage—almost to the breaking point.

Even as we left the hospital, grateful I had been delivered from a heart attack, we little dreamed that both of us—each in a different way—needed more healing from deep within.

Nor did we have the least idea of the struggles, griefs, and loneliness God would allow us to experience in order to bring us to the foot of the cross.

The day I left the hospital, however, found us facing nothing but "good problems." Should we continue our vacation as though nothing had interrupted it? Should we head for Warren Bryant's house?

Definitely. Even Anita didn't know how eager I was for her to become perfectly reconciled with her father.

What about Six Flags? Yes. The kids sure deserved it.

And how about High Flight?

No question. Jim Irwin described these POW and MIA families as some of America's most desperately needy people. He burned with Christian zeal towards them.

I also felt a tremendous burden for each of those heroes. Each one is a hero, of course, whether we're talking about a prisoner, for years systematically beaten and half-starved . . . a little kid who has grown up without his father . . . or a bewildered young wife with all the hope gone out of her eyes.

As usual, the Lord's timing was fantastic.

Anita was to sing and give her testimony. Despite her fatigue, she did a great job. But what struck both of us was how God used our experiences of that same week to help her minister to some very anguished people.

"I have had a glimpse of the kind of fear you wives and mothers have been living with," she told them. "I know how it feels to beg God to spare your husband's life.

"I know the terror of facing tomorrow without my husband at my side, the fear of having to rear four children without their father.

"But I also know that in the very blackest moments of pain and despair, my Jesus is present. In Proverbs 3:5–6, God tells us, 'Trust in the Lord with all thine heart; and lean not unto thine own understanding. In all thy ways acknowledge him, and he shall direct thy paths.' "

The High Flight retreats—there were a series of them, actually, throughout the summer—represented a mountain-top experience for us, literally and symbolically.

Colonel Irwin and his staff utilized the resources of a YMCA camp outside Denver to house capacity crowds. There were arts and crafts, horseback riding, and other great recreation for the kids. Their mothers and fathers, so newly reunited—or in many cases their mothers, despondent over the outlook for husbands still listed as "missing"—attended seminars, sharing groups, and counseling sessions.

Much to our delight, Teddy Heard flew in to conduct a seminar on "Creative Response to Stress." She, Anita, and I had a grand reunion at the Denver airport, with great hugging, prayer, praising, and some tears of joy. That was *our* creative response to stress.

Teddy and Anita had fantastic opportunities to share the Lord with numbers of distraught and empty women. Many of the wives had sustained themselves through Jesus the whole way. Others, however, were heartbreaking in their grief and bitterness and even anger at God.

Teddy and Anita very often drew apart to pray for one person or another, and they'd weep. You had to feel the really indescribable pain of people who face such terrible circumstances without the love and knowledge of Jesus Christ.

"There's such a difference where these gals have been able to relinquish their husband to the Lord," Anita told me. "I only had a few days of uncertainty and fear. These wives have lived with it for years."

One wife attended the First Baptist Church in Jacksonville, Florida, where the Reverend Homer Lindsay, our former pastor, is associate pastor with his father. Her faith and witness was so tremendous. She inspired Anita in a wonderful way.

By contrast, the women without faith so often felt confused, resentful, and bitter toward our country. They thought of themselves as forgotten people. It seemed as though when Jim Irwin's spiritual retreat was offered, it was the first evidence to them that someone cared after all.

Another thing we saw—and this was sobering—was the difference in kids' attitudes where the Lord was present in the home. Now that's true always, but especially in this extreme situation. So many of these kids with missing fathers seemed to hate their mothers. I didn't understand that at first, but then came to see it was because their mothers simply couldn't cope with this unnatural situation.

Only Jesus could make it possible to bear.

In other homes, the Lord had been able to take hostility, bitterness, fear, and depression out of the situation and allow the mothers to exhibit God's strength and comfort. It was interesting to see how adaptable and healthy the children from these homes seemed to be. These children showed no hatred toward their mothers.

The first evening of our stay, Anita was sharing with the mother of three teen-agers, a woman obviously in total despair. She broke down and wept bitterly as she told Anita about her faith in God—a faith which nevertheless didn't seem to offer sufficient comfort.

Anita soon discovered the woman had no personal relationship to Jesus Christ. She lacked those divine resources. She had made supreme efforts on her own, but a person can go only so far in his own strength.

Anita had the tremendous joy of leading this woman to the Lord. She trusted Jesus that evening—and from the depths of her despair, turned to Him who is the Way, the Truth and the Life.

It really was humbling to have the opportunity to testify from our own experiences about a Lord who wants to come into your life and live it with you; help you make tough decisions; bear your burdens; heal the brokenhearted; and take away all bitterness, substituting the divine love of God.

God hasn't promised to take away the terrible circumstances of life, but He has promised to give us every resource we need to obtain victory over *anything* this life can throw at us.

As I said, Anita really could witness with new power because of recent events in our own lives. The Holy Spirit used her to bring that needy woman to Christ.

"Oh, Bob, you should have seen how she looked," Anita said. "It amazed me how much she changed, even on the *outside*. All the sadness and pain vanished from her face.

"A look of such peace and joy came over her—a peace that's indescribable. Bob, she took on the radiance of Christ!"

And my wife wept with the joy of this woman's salvation.

So many others hungered and thirsted for Jesus, and those who knew Him labored mightily to minister to all who had needs. Anita counseled and prayed with several women who learned to trust Jesus, as a result.

Later, in a couple of instances, she received thanks and a follow-up by mail. One woman wrote that she still didn't know if her husband were alive or dead—but she knew Jesus is alive. You have to thank God when such faith springs to life in someone.

The spiritual retreat sponsored by High Flight became a real blessing to Anita and me. We went feeling great concern and wanting to minister, and so we did. Many people, however, were used of the Lord to minister to us.

As Anita wished, I kind of took things easy. I attended all her performances, but didn't attempt to do too much else. Gloria Roe flew in from California to accompany Anita, and did her usual great and sensitive job. Toward the end of our stay, Judge Wyatt Heard joined Teddy and the rest of us.

One evening the gals went to the grocery store and gathered provisions. We spent a few hours sprawled before the fireplace, rapping and toasting marshmallows, sharing anything and everything—Teddy and Wyatt, Gloria, Anita, and me. It was one of those spontaneous, beautiful times.

Because I was on medication, I didn't try to do much else. Denver's high altitude, I discovered, placed a certain strain on my system which made me glad to take it easy.

My considerable number of extra pounds became a liability in that mountainous terrain. An elevated blood pressure didn't help much, either.

Despite the blessings received, High Flight began to place me under some pressure—pressure I didn't want to admit to Anita or anyone else.

The tightness in my chest . . . the pressure and dizziness . . . had returned, along with considerable fear and apprehension.

I didn't know what to do.

Again and again I reached for my Bible and turned to Psalm 118—the one Teddy called "God's insurance policy."

# 8

# Glorify God in Your Body

I don't want to play up the heart thing.

It's not that important, except it was the first time my body ever scared me. It was a warning for Anita and me, and my doctor warned us further.

"You've got to change your life-style," he said. "Take off some of that weight. Get that blood pressure down. Learn how to cut down on tensions.

"It's *important.*"

The Lord had a purpose for that heart episode—several purposes. Today I look back and thank Him for that hassle, because it made me take a good look at my physical state. I could find no excuse for what I saw.

Yes, I thank God, because I was lucky. Many another man in his forties—even early forties, as was my case—doesn't get a second chance to shape up.

God created man in three parts; body, soul, and spirit. These parts intermingle in ways no scientist can explain. In the ideal human life, I'm sure the three facets of man would come into perfect balance.

Jesus, our example of perfect manhood, demonstrated that balance.

74

The rest of us appear to concentrate on one aspect of our lives to the neglect of others, it seems to me. Far too many Americans, certainly, ignore their run-down bodies.

That was the case with me. In my years of discouragement —being unable to diet successfully—I had actually *prayed* to the Lord that He *shake* me into taking care of my body— and He did!

In the hospital, however, I noticed how skinny all the cardiologists were. That was a sermon in itself!

Back home, I got serious about my physical fitness. The first thing I did was quit eating like a hog, and I lost forty-three pounds. I got motivated. Nothing else had worked, before this, but now nobody had to nag me to lose weight.

I also started reading Christian books on diet and exercise. I bought a book on aerobics and determined to get back in shape.

Aerobics is a form of exercise which forces the body to consume increased amounts of oxygen and as such is the only form of exercise that benefits not just the skeletal muscles but the whole body. There are several good books about this program and one of them is *The New Aerobics* by Kenneth H. Cooper. It contains the program that has been officially adopted by the United States Air Force—that's how good this conditioning method is.

It wasn't easy. The first time I tested myself on aerobics I found I couldn't run a mile, but had to walk some, then run a bit, then walk some more, and so on. It was terrible.

So many people begin a good exercise program, but don't stick with it. I decided to keep daily records, carrying a stopwatch, and recording my heartbeats per minute. These records show gradual but steady improvements, and keep me going when I get discouraged.

Another unnerving thing was the way I could hear myself

gasping for breath whenever I stopped running. I wanted to shut out my gasps, so I got a little head-hugger radio. With a tennis cap and this radio on my head, I run to a radio in the mornings, and I have to carry a stick because of the dogs. They really take off after me!

As I describe these humorous-sounding situations, it's hard to convey the real sense of panic—even despair—I sometimes felt. For one thing, the physical fitness bit very often is something a man gets into by himself. It's a lonely undertaking at best, frustrating at worst—and there's a constant temptation to chuck the whole thing.

So when I get up in the morning, I include a goodly portion of prayer, having set the alarm clock very early—an hour before anyone else gets up—and then I run one mile and sometimes two miles. While I am running, I am praying and praising the Lord, so that when I come back, my mind is clear and I have fully awakened. Then I read the Bible and everything is illuminated for me. Since I have started the exercise, my headaches have disappeared and my blood pressure is down to normal—and of course I have lost forty-three pounds! At the start of my jogging program I couldn't run a straight mile. I had to run and walk a mile in about twenty minutes and now I am running a mile in seven minutes, and running two miles in fifteen minutes. The most important thing is that my pulse recovery rate dropped down immediately upon the stopping of the exercise and it very quickly comes back to normal. My pulse rate at rest averages in mid-forties, whereas before it was averaging in the mid-eighties. In addition to this jogging, I am now able to play an hour of tennis singles daily. The most important thing is that before going into any exercise program a person should get a complete physical, and if you are forty or over, it is essential that the electrocardiogram be made under stress.

There was an interesting article about this in the September, 1974, issue of *Reader's Digest,* "The Heart Test That Could Save Your Life" by Arlene and Howard Isenberg, condensed from *Parade* magazine. According to Dr. Irving M. Levitas who is quoted in the article, each year more than one million Americans are knocked out by heart attacks, many within weeks or days after passing standard ECGs. He points out that some physicians continue to test hearts with the patient flat on his back since many people with coronary disease actually show normal resting ECGs. "You have to test the heart the way you do a car. Take it out on the highway and let it ping," the doctor declared. The new exercises are performed on a stationary bicycle or treadmill while a cardiologist monitors your heart continuously and stops if there is an abnormal ECG or blood-pressure reading. Levitas urges men and women to inquire about this method of testing and indicates that some day it may become a routine part of every thorough physical exam. "The scary thing is that possibly one in every ten American males, and a growing amount of females between the ages of thirty and sixty are probably walking around with unsuspected, unrecognized coronary diseases," the doctor said.

This means that approximately ten thousand of the males reading this book are walking around with coronary artery diseases! Of course, the very main thing is that any exercise program is thoroughly checked out with your doctor beforehand.

Here's where a good wife can really help a man. She can understand, sympathize, and encourage him. She can realize how vitally important his health and well-being really are to her, their children, and the community.

The Bible, of course, emphasizes the importance of reverencing one's body. First Corinthians 6:19, 20 says: "What? know ye not that your body is the temple of the Holy Ghost which is in you, which ye have of God, and ye are not your own?

"For ye are bought with a price: therefore glorify God in your body, and in your spirit, which are God's."

Few people *really* regard their bodies as temples of the Holy Spirit. I never had, certainly. But when you begin to consider your physical self as God planned for you to operate —a marvel of construction and performance—it takes on a different light. It sure helps you understand, for example, that gluttony is sinful.

I never had much of a victory over gluttony, because I never really wanted to turn that over to the Lord. I liked eating, and ate all the wrong things for all the wrong reasons. Again, this is a place where a wife can help a husband learn something about self-control.

Sure, it's hard. Anita has yelled at me so many times for eating forbidden foods and then I'd get mad at her. But it's important to keep on yelling. Somehow that man has got to curb that killer appetite.

Why does anyone overeat? Many an American needs to be wrestling with that question right this moment. If you are overweight—and if you plan to conquer that sin, with God's help—the first question to ask yourself is *why*.

Know thyself. Keep a record of everything you eat, and the time of day during which you consume foods, and watch for patterns. Do you eat because you're tense? Tired? Bored? Resentful? Ask Jesus to help you know *why you eat*. Then ask Him to help you break your destructive eating patterns. This He will do, because He desires your perfect health.

If you or someone else in your family has a problem of overweight, I urge you to stop reading right now and turn the whole thing over to Christ. Ask Him to show you the seriousness of your sin. Ask Him to give you grace to change your habits even as He grants the insights which bring these areas of cheating and deception to your mind.

Yes—cheating. Show me a fat person, and I'll show you a food cheat and, in all probability, a liar. Very few of us are willing to admit to gluttony. We shade the quantity and quality of our sins, persuading ourselves that it really doesn't matter.

How can God help us if we persist in such head-in-the-sand practices? No wonder gluttony is listed as one of the seven deadly sins, when you consider how it dulls mind, body, and spirit.

Anita says there's nobody in the world quite so virtuous as a reformed foodoholic. Probably so. In my own case, losing forty-three pounds was something I never could have done without the Lord's help. Admittedly, however, it helped also to get scared by a heart flare-up.

You grow up thinking of the heart as the body's most important organ. And then, perhaps, you experience the pain, erratic heartbeat, chest tightness or any of a dozen other heart-disease symptoms.

Whenever I'm tempted to forget diet and exercise, two thoughts invariably turn me back toward my disciplines. One is my memory of the catheterization procedure. You see them place a tube in your groin and you look up at the monitor to see it snaking up through your vein, see it entering your heart, and then they ask you to breathe deeply, cough, and do other things necessary for the test.

My other very effective thought concerns my memory of

Anita on that morning prior to my catheterization. I see her walking into my room, wearing the Florida citrus-colored dress and doing the make-Bob-feel-cheerful number. I get a kick out of that, because it's Anita all the way. The yellow dress, the big smile, the big hello. . . .

But of course that was *not* just Anita. It was her fantastic faith in operation.

Anita and I really claim Romans 8:28 in our daily lives. We believe all things *do* work together for good, and even when we could tell the doctors were sure there was something wrong with me—we could praise the Lord.

We learned some things about our emotions, too.

Anita learned two main facts: that she's enormously dependent on me, and also that she's perfectly capable of hanging in there herself. She did superwell during those bad days in Tulsa.

Our experience taught me not to try to do all the coping. I really think I had been a plastic man until that point.

I also learned that the human being adapts very well. The world does not end if your physical self changes drastically. That's an amazing fact for a man, in particular, to discover.

Another thing I learned was that at a time of crisis I could lean on Jesus. I wasn't worried about my kids' care, nor was I at any time concerned for Bob Green personally. I learned I really did trust the Lord.

But though I was sedated, and knew no agony, I experienced a physical feeling I'd never known before, a feeling I had no way of relieving. The pain just wouldn't go away. I discovered I was a big baby as far as any physical discomfort was concerned.

Back home, with my diet, exercise, and medication right on target so far as we knew, things should have gone great.

Instead, I found myself succumbing to terrible fits of fear and depression—because the symptoms of former trouble had returned.

No mistake. I kept having this ringing in the ears and other unpleasant symptoms. I'd be sitting in church with my heart beating wildly. There would be tightness in the chest, and I'd break out in a cold sweat.

Eventually I began to think they had made a drastic mistake in Tulsa. I waited for weeks for those unpleasant physical manifestations to vanish, but they grew increasingly worse. I couldn't go to a movie . . . couldn't enjoy myself at church . . . or participate with the family.

Anita, meanwhile, kept harping on one idea: *There was nothing wrong with my heart.* Specialists in Tulsa had agreed on that. She wanted me to get my mind off myself and back to more normal preoccupations. She began to get tense and withdrawn, and she obviously resented my health measures —especially the jogging.

Why couldn't she see it was essential?

"You're not sick, Bob," she reminded me at least once a day. "Your tests proved your heart is okay. They told us you are perfectly well, and if you *aren't* well—see another doctor! But you're getting so self-centered nobody can stand you. You're concentrating on *self, self, self.* You're only interested in your own heartbeat, your own symptoms.

"Face it, Bob. You're a hypochondriac!"

I resented that. I knew my ill feelings were perfectly valid; Anita evidently considered they existed only in my mind.

Each day found me dreading the onset of rapid heartbeat, tightness in the chest, the familiar clammy hands.

When I'd complain, however, I got rage instead of sympathy.

"Bob! Quit complaining—see a doctor. There's nothing

wrong with you—nothing physical, at least," she'd say. "Tests prove that, Bob."

I thought I must be losing my mind. I'd always thought I had control over my mind, but I got to the point where I knew I was headed for a nervous breakdown.

Depressed to the point of despair, living in constant fear and anxiety, Bob Green found he no longer could cope. I spent long days brooding about things I didn't dare do. Panic frequently overtook me, pain flared up increasingly often, and I lived in dread of experiencing a massive heart attack.

Nor could I pray about it. You can get so low you don't even have energy to pray—even to save your life.

It was at that point that Teddy Heard stepped in with some sensible advice. "Maybe you need more tests," she suggested. "Why not consult another heart specialist?"

Anita, meanwhile, had just about had it. My convalescence had lasted so long—had been so ineffectual—and showed no signs of victory. What would you think in those circumstances?

Fortunately, Anita (who all along had begged me to see a doctor) seized on Teddy's suggestion. My illness (she thought it was pseudoillness) bothered her so much we began making arrangements to send me to the Mayo Clinic.

Before going to Mayo Clinic, however, I decided to consult a specialist at the Miami Heart Institute. Maybe he could find a clue.

I arrived at his office in deplorable condition, filled with fear, experiencing ringing in the ears, dizziness, pain.

"In Tulsa they told me you have a perfect heart," Anita reminded me again.

I was beginning to doubt my sanity.

The symptoms were very real, but I had been told I was

perfectly well. Obviously I was headed for a nervous break-down.

What happened next almost sounds anticlimactic.

My specialist almost immediately diagnosed my problem as "hyperdynamic myocardiopathy"—a big mouthful that means there's something in the system that makes the heart beat faster and give all the symptoms of a heart attack.

The disease sounds terrible. Actually, it's curable, with medication and exercise. I felt relieved and elated past belief to learn it simply was a matter of prescribing some pills. The disease eventually would respond, my doctor assured me. I could expect a cure in six months or so, with luck—maybe as long as six years, otherwise. Meanwhile, medication would keep it under control.

I could hardly believe my ears. For the first time, I felt real hope. But could we really believe the diagnosis? It was hard to hope for a cure after all those weeks and months. . . .

"That's it, okay," the doctor said, confidently. "I heard it when I listened to the heart. Before that, I felt 99 percent sure from reading the tapes from Tulsa."

Why had the Tulsa doctors overlooked the problem?

"It's not a well-known disease," he told me. "We get all kinds of cases here from all over the world, so we see much more of it than the ordinary facility would encounter.

"Today a young All-American football player came in with these same symptoms."

He scribbled a prescription, and I hurried to get it filled. That evening, after the first pills, we could go out for pizza and shopping. I was normal again.

Praise the Lord! I keep thinking there are men all over the country who think they have heart problems, when it could be something relatively simple.

My experience makes me urge them to seek a heart specialist if real heart symptoms occur. Go to a cardiologist and get
an electrocardiogram, made *under stress.*

During those stress-filled weeks, I thought my prayers
were unselfish. I prayed that if God would heal me, with
whatever strength I had I'd focus on working for Him.

"Especially on Fishers of Men Opportunities, Lord," I
promised. Gratefully I recalled my promises to the Lord. I
could hardly wait to start working for Him!

# 9

# Trust the Lord

God truly had prepared me for a tough time.

Months earlier, I had made a covenant with the Lord that I would praise Him in all things. Through my praise, He has shown me so much!

Teddy always was praising God, and her life showed the effects. She felt her special ministry was to show the joy of the Lord. Bob called Teddy a "swinging Christian."

Teddy had something special, as does Marabel Morgan. I wanted their kind of Christian radiance.

My daily devotions begin at six A.M., at the little chair beside my desk in the kitchen. That's holy ground. I kneel there to pray, and I keep my Bible and *My Utmost For His Highest* (my favorite book of devotions) beside me at all times.

My power source is that daily discipline of prayer, confessing any known sin, reading the Word, asking the Holy Spirit to fill me and take over my will, intellect, emotions, and entire body to prepare me for the day. By the time the kids come downstairs I have prayed for each of them, for Bob and myself, and for God's work that day.

That is my key to readiness.

Without those habits, I somehow doubt I could have made it through the events which followed. Fortunately for all of us, I had learned to "trust in the Lord with all my heart, and lean not unto my own understanding" (*see* Proverbs 3:5).

That trust was to serve me well.

"Anita, Bob's going to have a rough time when he gets home," Gloria said. "This heart thing is one of the worst times he's ever known.

"You'd better prepare yourself for what comes next. I believe that when Bob gets back into home territory he's going to become totally wrapped up in his own body."

I should have paid more attention to Gloria Roe Robertson's insight. Gloria, a concert pianist, singer, and composer of sacred music, often accompanies me when I perform. She is my Christian sister, and she helped lead Bob to the Lord.

"Oftentimes a heart attack hits a man psychologically," she continued. "Bob didn't have an attack, of course, but the damage is done, where his psyche is concerned. He thinks his body has betrayed him."

I heard Gloria's words, but dismissed them. I thought she was being overly fearful.

Boy, was she right!

Back home, I watched as Bob seemed to revert to exactly the same symptoms he'd had before. Doctors in Tulsa had given him a clean bill of health, but obviously he didn't believe them.

It seemed to me he deliberately psyched himself back down into that fear and panic, and brought the same physical symptoms back.

Gradually our way of life changed as Bob became increasingly more preoccupied with his problems. He began skipping breakfast so as to have time for jogging. Always breakfast time was special for all of us—a consecrated beginning of our day.

Bob and I had taken pains to establish certain customs—Bible reading before the kids left for school, a brief prayer, and Bob would read a daily selection from *Little Visits With God*. The kids love that book.

Billy Graham believes in family devotions and he and Ruth established a very similar pattern for their children. We had followed their lead, and felt it paid off.

Now nothing seemed right, because Daddy always was absent from the breakfast table. More importantly, we all felt the lack of his spiritual leadership. I felt he set a good example for his kids—yet now, suddenly, he was throwing it all overboard. He didn't seem to care about us anymore.

I broke my neck to care for him—special diets and all—but thought only of what *I* was enduring. I didn't understand at all what Bob was going through. He seemed so totally self-absorbed, so unbelievably remote at times. . . .

What could be done? I tried and tried to establish communication between us, but our relationship became more and more strained. Had I not established that pattern of morning worship and praise for myself, we never could have survived.

Concerned for his health in the beginning, I eventually grew to consider the whole thing intolerable. Everything suffered—his roughhousing with the kids, family meals, our lovemaking. Bob's every action seemed dominated by his fear of having a heart attack. Though I could understand this intellectually, my emotions could not accept the situation.

So we slowly grew apart.

It's important to explain here that Bob and I maintained —during these long and difficult weeks—faithful prayer lives. Gradually we entered into a period of virtual estrangement from one another, thanks to the physical condition which seemed to obsess my husband. Nevertheless, each in his own way continued his prayer disciplines. Without that anchor I feel certain our marriage would have drifted too far in the wrong direction.

But God honors prayer. The Bible says in James 5:16 that the fervent prayer of a rightous man availeth much—and we were to learn the truth in that!

For some time, the Lord gave me a special understanding of Bob's needs. I tried to fill in for his absences. More and more I handled household affairs normally considered his. And always I tried to give the kids extra attention, lest they miss their daddy too much, and suffer.

The Holy Spirit filled me daily with the grace of God. Eventually, however, fatigue and resentment overtook me. Bob continued to complain of pain and other symptoms, yet refused to see a doctor. He was impossible!

Resentments . . . frustrations . . . Bob's concern for his body . . . these problems gradually began to swamp us. Had it not been for the love of the Lord, I would have snapped.

Yet I took good care of him. I looked after his special diet, tried to make him comfortable in every way, and assumed full responsibility for all the children.

Also during this time I was experiencing pain in different parts of my body and real heaviness in my gums and had speech problems. At first I panicked but turned it over to the Lord. My dentist said it was a vitamin deficiency which was caused by great stress. (He was so right!) It could be corrected within a few weeks with proper diet and vitamins, he said.

Worst of all, I faced surgery myself. Any woman would understand my anxiety over cysts in the breasts. Tired and psychologically down, I felt less than up to the emotional challenge such surgery presented. I dreaded bad news—especially if I had to face it alone. The surgeon was fairly sure everything would be all right, but they are never positive until they operate.

I should not have underestimated my husband. Bob takes such good care of me always, and this time was no exception. He became so sweet, so concerned, ministered to me and ordered beautiful flowers—and made sure my name got on the church prayer list.

The Lord led me to do something unusual the day before I entered the hospital. Feeling really unhappy about the surgery, tired and off stride physically and emotionally, I knew I needed something extra.

I asked my friend Dan Topping, who even then was sadly incapacitated by the emphysema which took his life, to pray for me. That seemed to thrill Dan—the knowledge that someone else needed him. I guess it helped him get outside his own tedious and relentless problems.

Not only did Dan pray for me, he also sent some gorgeous flowers to my hospital room, and he visited me there as well. I needed a friend. It really blessed my heart to know that Dan, by then far weaker and certainly more ill than me, would make all that effort for me.

Bob and I consider that one of our sweetest memories of Dan Topping, a fine gentleman and good friend whom we'd helped lead to the Lord. Charlotte, his wife, is one of the first persons I ever helped come to Christ. She is my true Christian sister, and I treasure her—and their five children, too.

God blessed me in that surgery. Everything was okay, nothing malignant, and all went well. Bob's concern and attentiveness fed my starved self, and for a few days I lapped up all the attention.

Gradually, however, we returned to the kind of life which had somehow become normal for us. Bob devoted himself to business, jogging, diet, medication, and bad moods. I majored in the kids, cooking, working on the book, trying to alter Bob's moods, and feeling enormous amounts of self-pity.

We had reached a stalemate. Nothing seemed to move. What would get us off dead center?

Somehow I sensed that the key person in this situation was *me*—that somehow I should be able to change things. Did I pray enough? Did I truly turn my husband over to the Lord? Did I trust Jesus to heal our situation?

More important, maybe—did I have the gift of long-suffering? I wanted to be patient—*tried* to be patient—but sometimes it was too much. I'd yell at Bob or snap at him before I thought. The situation was really miserable.

Then, remorseful, I'd phone Teddy and weep over what a bad wife Bob had. I'd feel these great waves of gratitude to God for sparing his life, then in the next moment say something nasty to Bob.

My point in sharing these things is simply this: I know that only the grace of God protected Bob Green and me during a long year of stress and continued assaults on our relationship.

Without Christ, that marriage could not have remained intact. Certainly there was no grace within Bob or me that could help the situation. We had gone way beyond our depth, and at times felt as though we were drowning in all the stress, weariness, unhappiness, fear—and loneliness.

Jesus never promised us happiness, of course. In fact, he

promised us tribulations; but he also promised *joy*. That daily discipline of devotion I'd entered into much earlier began to yield a strange kind of joy—the knowledge that of myself I could do nothing, but that God would supply all my needs in Christ Jesus.

*Joy!* I guess you have to get really down before you can look up and see it. Happiness is a man-made thing. Joy comes from our Father above.

Why did Bob and I suffer such estrangment from one another? Why did communication between us virtually vanish, and hostility replace our normal camaraderie? Why could we not express our feelings and our fears?

Why did I not understand that my husband lived in fear of an imminent heart seizure? That he felt real symptoms of real disease? Why did I continually call him neurotic, self-centered, a hypochondriac?

Bob and I grew more and more cold and destructive toward one another. We had entered a period of relentless personal testing. Nothing but faith could have carried me through those frustrating and frightening days, and I know that's true in Bob's case, too.

We knew nothing to do except trust the Lord and keep on keeping on. Of course, that's always the thing to do.

I guess it surprised us to see that even Christ-centered marriages can be attacked from within, and that we are not immune to the world's ills.

But we also learned that Christ is the Light at the end of any dark tunnel—and both of us followed His gleam. With Job I could say, "Though [God] slay me, yet will I trust in him" (13:15).

I was to need even more trust. Other dark days followed —days of soul struggle. It was to be a long, long time before

I could, with the Apostle Paul, say that "whatsoever state I'm in, therewith will I be content" (*see* Philippians 4:11).

When God lights your candle, however, even Satan himself cannot extinguish that holy flame. The Christian who knows that, and who truly loves the Lord, can praise Him even for those dark nights of the soul.

God, teach us to trust. Teach us to praise!

# Anita

# 10
# Step of Faith

During the difficult months I just described, Teddy Heard truly became my ministering angel.

I telephoned her almost every day—from Miami Beach to Houston, yet!—and the Jesus in Teddy embraced me and comforted my soul.

This gal possessed so many rare qualities.

She literally had been fed God's Word from cradle days. Her parents taught her to seek answers to all life's problems in the Holy Bible. No wonder she had such wholeness, freedom, and a creative approach to life the rest of us envied but did not totally understand, and yet Teddy was very human and many times shared her own problems and disappointments with me. It gave me great joy to be in a position to meet some of her needs, too.

Her calmness, clear thinking and wisdom of the Lord combined with a fantastic sense of fun—made problem-solving seem like terrific adventure.

Teddy, like me, not only saw potential problems in Bob's having an office in our home, but said so.

"When do either of you have any privacy?" she asked.

"Sure your house is big enough to include an office for Bob, but I wonder if you should.

"Seems to me Bob gets involved in household decisions, you in his office work, and boundaries cease to exist. I'm for boundaries, Anita," she said in her straightforward way. "If I were you, I'd kick Bob out."

Bob knew exactly what Teddy meant, and he loved her for it. We both saw the wisdom in her suggestion, especially since we stayed so tense these days. If Bob had his office elsewhere, that should defuse some of those explosive situations.

The trouble was, I did but didn't want him to go. Some childish—or perhaps motherly—streak in me wanted to have Bob at arm's reach, instantly available whenever I hollered. On the other hand, there'd be days when we bickered so much and he was such a pain that I just wanted to yell, "Get out!"

Teddy encouraged Bob and me to talk over the whole thing sensibly. We decided a new office for Bob would benefit us, the kids, the household, and Bob's business.

When we prayed about it, the Lord confirmed our decision. So Bob started looking for a downtown office location —a real step of faith, believe me.

You see, whether or not he'd admit it, Bob struggled daily with the heaviest depression he ever had known. He continued to experience frightening heart flare-ups. His new life-style completely changed his metabolism, which created another terrific adjustment for him, and his mind stayed fixed on morbid ideas a lot of the time.

Nevertheless, Bob did promise God he would devote his remaining life to Christian work. Though he literally had no heart for making any kind of major change, God gave him the go-ahead anyhow.

Therefore, on faith, Bob moved into a spacious, handsome office building at 3050 Biscayne Boulevard, Suite 1004, in Miami. He proceeded to furnish his new quarters with really elegant stuff. Despite our low morale, we couldn't help getting excited about it.

"I'm getting to know a side of you I never saw before," I told him. "Your office tells me so much about you. I'd never have guessed you'd choose furnishings like these."

"Like it?" he asked, real casually, as if he didn't care.

"Sure I do! I guess you're a lot more creative—and sort of breezy or something—than I knew."

He laughed. "Sure I'm creative. Why not? You just stick around, baby, and watch what happens with Fishers of Men Opportunities."

"Oh, Bob, you *know* the Holy Spirit gave you that idea! Let's just pray right now, and dedicate your office to everything the Lord had in mind. I'm so proud of you!"

Fishers of Men Opportunities, Inc., uniquely fulfills Bob's special abilities. It's got to be the most creative idea he ever had, and Bob's a real idea man.

Essentially, he saw the need for a special kind of talent agency—a Christian agency—which could provide speakers, musicians, politicians, athletes, all sorts of interesting Christian personalities, for churches and other religious organizations who need them.

Super! It took plenty of work and organization, but Bob got the business under way. When we mentioned this new baby in an earlier book, the dam really burst. He has been flooded with requests for Christian talent ever since.

Now, since his illness, work had stacked up. Bob and his secretary, established now in the scrumptious new office God provided, lit into the work. Everything looked great.

When you'd share good news with Teddy, often she'd respond with some happy phrase from the Bible. She knew God's Word so well that a verse or so of lovely Scripture would spring to her lips as fast as a song might come to mine.

She sounded so loving, so excited, when I told her about Bob's happiness.

"Bless the Lord, oh, my soul, and all that is within me bless His holy Name!" she exclaimed fervently. "Do tell Bob we love him. We're just going to lift up Fishers of Men before God in all our prayers. He's *really* going to use Bob. Oh, praise the Lord!" she exclaimed, her voice filled with delight.

"Teddy, Bob's office really turned out to be expensive. As you know, Fishers of Men won't be a big money-maker for Bob. He didn't set it up that way. It's not a question of money or anything like that, but I do keep wondering. About the office: Do you think Bob ran ahead of the Lord?"

"Oh, Anita, of course not," Teddy gently reproved me. "You *know* God knows all these things. . . ."

"Oh, sure."

" . . . well, I just know He *loves* Bob's new office!"

You had to love her for the way she loved Him. It hurt, therefore, to phone Teddy one day and absolutely drop a bombshell about Fishers of Men.

"Teddy, Bob's been operating without a license. He didn't dream he had to have one—there's very little profit involved for him—but now they're making him close down. I can't believe it! The new office—all the beautiful furniture—he just loves it, and this makes me sick. Bob has to apply for an agency license. What if they don't give him one?"

It is tough going but Bob faithfully jogs two miles every morning before going to work. *Below:* Around the breakfast table.

Bob leads the bicycle parade. *Below:* Yes, when the Greens go grocery shopping we need two carts, and usually more!

Gloria and Barbara help me in the kitchen. *Below:* Sometimes the best meal is an impromptu picnic in our courtyard.

Bobby thinks Bob has relaxed enough! *Below:* Time for touch football.

Billy gets pinned by his big brother. *Below:* After all that exercise it's time for a dip.

Meanwhile Bob and Bobby try their luck at fishing off our dock. *Below:* It's time for me to prepare for my Sunday-school class. Those glasses do help me see the fine print in God's Word!

Mother (Grandma Kate) supervises quiet playtime. *Right:* Billy and Barbara struggle for the microphone while Bob and Gloria play a piano duet. Bobby and Anita prepare to sing or direct.

Bobby is learning to play the organ quite well. *Below:* Family television hour at Villa Verde—I prefer my needlepoint.

Bible and prayers at the family altar at bedtime.

Bob and I entertain Dick and Janie Beeler. We met Janie at Teddy's funeral. (She provided the plane from Houston to Stetson University.) *Below:* Sunday finds us at Northwest Baptist Church in North Miami.

I explain Teddy's trinity to my eleven-year-olds at Sunday school. *Right:* We hold hands in a prayer circle as we pray for the special needs of one of the class members.

Jerry Kranz teaches Billy's Sunday-school class. *Below:* This picture of our family with Evangelist J. Harold Smith, Governor Reubin Askew, and Brother Bill was taken after the services outside of Northwest Baptist.

I visit with Frank Gleman and his granddaughter, Alex Sheenan, at the church before their baptism. *Below:* The twins and I model at a Project Survival Luncheon.

Mike Douglas and I belt out a song on the "Mike Douglas Show." *Below:* Bob invites me to view his new office, the home of Bob Green Productions and Fishers of Men, Incorporated.

Another view of Bob's new office. *Below:* On the evening of Teddy's funeral I shared the events of her "graduation exercise" with the students of Stetson University in DeLand, Florida.

My beloved sister in Christ, Teddy Moody Heard.

"Anita, you *know* they will."

"Teddy, this is Miami. Talent is such big business . . . and despite the fact that Bob hasn't profited personally from his agency work, they might make him close down. They don't understand about this being a Christian ministry, or maybe it's just that they don't care. What if they make Bob give up Fishers of Men?"

"Praise the Lord, Anita! If the devil has attacked Bob already, he must really hate what Bob's trying to do. Isn't that *wonderful?*"

I wished I could share her enthusiasm.

"Teddy," I said again, with even more emphasis. "Please don't celebrate. I'm telling you Bob needs a license, and they might not grant him one!"

"Don't be silly!" she responded gaily. "Not give God a license for His work? They wouldn't *dare*. Let's just pray about it right now. Isn't God good!"

You had to relax and rejoice with her. She had the most direct pipeline to heaven I ever saw, and kept it in constant use. "Let's just pray about that" came to her lips as spontaneously as "thank you," and her conversations with God were alive with tender expressions of love and gratitude.

"Father, we just praise Your Name," she began. "We thank You that Bob is experiencing the kind of opposition that makes him know You mean business. . . ."

A somewhat unorthodox prayer, maybe. But the kind that reveals so much individuality—trust—faith in God's purposes.

So I began to thank God for Bob's new office, and for the step of faith it had represented for him. And I thanked God for Teddy, and for her little quickie prayers about anything and everything that came up.

Each prayer, I realized, amounted to another step of faith
—steps which hour by hour enable a Christian to walk close
to Jesus.

Thank God for love in action! Thank God for those who
step out in His Name!

# *Anita*

## II
# Blessings

Ask, and it shall be given you; seek, and ye shall find; knock, and it shall be opened unto you:

For every one that asketh receiveth; and he that seeketh findeth; and to him that knocketh it shall be opened.

*Matthew 7:7, 8*

Do you believe those words?

Jesus said them! That is enough.

When you learn to claim the promises of our blessed Lord —claiming them when you feel hopeless, claiming when you feel nothing at all—*that* is when faith makes all things possible.

Again and again God showed Bob and me His amazing grace during times when of ourselves we could do nothing.

As Psalms 145:8, 9 says: "The Lord is gracious, and full of compassion; slow to anger, and of great mercy. The Lord is good to all: and his tender mercies are over all his works."

Often His mercies make our hearts overflow. I'm thinking of the Sunday only a few weeks after Bob's heart seizure

*99*

when he, with two other laymen, Bob Hall and Charles Mathis from the Northwest Baptist Church in North Miami, were ordained as deacons.

We wives (Suzanne Hall, Linda Mathis, and I) stood behind our husbands during the ceremony as, with the laying on of hands, the men were given that special ministry and responsibility Paul described to Timothy:

> Likewise must the deacons be grave, not doubletongued, not given to much wine, not greedy of filthy lucre;
>
> Holding the mystery of the faith in a pure conscience.
>
> And let these also first be proved; then let them use the office of a deacon, being found blameless.
>
> Even so must their wives be grave, not slanderers, sober, faithful in all things.
>
> Let the deacons be the husbands of one wife, ruling their children and their own houses well.
>
> For they that have used the office of a deacon well purchase to themselves a good degree, and great boldness in the faith which is in Christ Jesus.
>
> 1 Timothy 3:8–13

For me, this was a dream come true. I felt proud and excited, touched, and deeply humbled. Brother Bill Chapman, our pastor, really loves Bob. He often remarks on how Bob truly loves the Lord, and how fast he is growing in the faith. Brother Bill has a gift for seeing your spiritual potential and, with his perception and encouragement, brings out beautiful new talents for the Lord.

That day I watched through tear-filled eyes as he beamed at our three new deacons, loving them, thrilled with the significance of the step they had just taken for Jesus. I thank God my husband had that privilege—that He and the deacon committee saw fit to bestow that blessing on us.

Several weeks later the Reverend John Huffman of the Key Biscayne Presbyterian Church invited me to sing and give my testimony before his congregation. At that time, Brother Huffman and his church were often in the news, because President Richard M. Nixon attended his church when vacationing in Key Biscayne.

Now John and his wife, Anne, had accepted a new pastorate and would be leaving Miami, so we wanted to visit his church. Before the service, John asked Bob to give his testimony before I gave mine.

Bob believes in witnessing—especially when he can push *me* out there and make me do it! Recently, however, he has been really good about speaking out for the Lord. More and more he's willing to give his own testimony.

Bob's voice trembled as he told how God had put him down, had brought him low in physical weakness, and had used those circumstances to strip him of pride.

"That's the only way I could accept the calling as deacon in our church," Bob confessed. "First, God had to break me. He had to make me conscious of my weakness and willing to be totally dependent on Him.

"I thank God I have no strength apart from Him."

That was the first time Bob publicly shared our most recent struggles. It was so sweet. Watching him fight to maintain his composure, listening to the quiver in his voice, I admit my eyes filled up.

Many people came forward that day to tell Bob he had blessed their hearts. Once again I was struck by the very marvelous way God makes redemptive use out of anything we turn over to Him. Already Bob was using those fearful experiences to glorify God and praise His Name!

And then, one sparkling weekend in October, we found ourselves scheduled to attend Homecoming festivities at Baylor University in Waco, Texas. Now this really was something offbeat, for me, spending a social weekend—a long one, at that—away from home and the kids. I couldn't remember another occasion like it.

Teddy Heard, of course, was responsible. Wyatt, a loyal Baylor alumnus, is still a little bit fanatical about his college. "Especially the football team," Teddy confided, explaining that Wyatt is a football scout.

Wyatt had invited us to Homecoming especially so I'd sing and give my testimony to the students at their chapel. I felt hesitant about agreeing. I never finished college, and always have some feelings of inadequacy where speaking to college groups is concerned. On the other hand, Teddy had done so many, many favors for me. . . .

"If you really want to do something for me, do this for Wyatt," Teddy suggested. "Come to Baylor. It's so important to Wyatt that you witness to these precious students!"

Praise the Lord, we went. Bob and Wyatt watched the football game, I assume. Teddy and I attended with them, but I'm afraid we talked more yards than the players gained. It reminded me of the first time Teddy and I accompanied our husbands to a Miami Dolphins game. Her enthusiasm impressed me so much.

"Do you really love football?" I asked, enviously.

"Let's just say I love Wyatt Heard," she said, laughing mischievously.

Before going to church the next day, someone had asked me to sing and give my testimony, but I had declined, explaining that another church previously asked and I had refused them.

Accordingly, the four of us were sitting way in the back of the church. Then Bob passed me a note which said he felt an urgent leading for me to go forward and give my testimony after all and that it would be a waste and hiding the Gospel if I didn't! I couldn't believe it; I gave him an unusually dirty look.

"Too late!" I whispered to Bob. "The service is set. We can't break into it now!"

Wyatt overheard us. He intercepted the note, indicating that it wasn't too late after all. He summoned an usher and sent a message to the pulpit. To my intense embarrassment, I was invited to come forward and speak.

That was the longest aisle I ever walked. The church was packed, and everybody watched me trudge forward. At the podium, I just leveled with them.

"I really don't know what to say," I began. "My husband arranged all this. *He's* the one who volunteered me. . . ." I got a naughty little satisfaction from making Bob squirm (I hope) in his seat. However, I went on from there with my witness, and the Lord supplied the words. As usual, He gave me what I needed and I sang a song a capella.

The next day really had me worried. I was to speak at the Monday morning chapel service, and my time would be strictly limited.

"You have forty minutes, and then the students walk out on you," Wyatt said.

*Walk out?* I felt horrified.

"Afraid so. They have to get to their next class. . . ."

That was understandable. But how, on the other hand, could I observe a time limit? My witness and songs always go as the Holy Spirit directs, but this time I seemed to feel *I* needed to control the time factor. I felt extremely scared about the whole thing.

In the dressing room before chapel period, Teddy led Kurt Kaiser, Bob, Wyatt, and me in prayer. Kurt Kaiser had consented to play piano for me since we were in Word Records' hometown and would be recording the service for a future album. After the prayer, I felt nervousness slide away like a heavy coat slipping off my shoulders.

The Lord *did* control the length of my testimony. I spoke exactly the right amount of time—to the minute. There was no fear. Instead, I spoke easily and confidently to a sweet and attentive audience, and then they gave me a standing ovation. I couldn't believe it!

Afterwards my dressing room became an altar. Two kids were saved and others rededicated their lives as a result of the service.

That was a powerful weekend, and we'll always remember it. And then there was the weekend Teddy flew down and visited me. I had a convention booked in Boca Raton, Florida, and this time Bob let Teddy and me drive over to the booking without him. That's very, very unusual. Normally he takes me wherever I go. This was nearby, however, and I guess he thought Teddy and I would have a great time together—which was true. We did.

We drove back singing at the tops of our lungs—songs like "Alleluia," "Old Rugged Cross," and "There's a Sweet, Sweet Spirit in This Place."

Speaking of bookings, the Lord sent us a mighty unusual one in Syracuse, New York. Don Sanders, a leading layman in a community church there, hired me to do a show in a local hotel. He paid my usual fee for me to perform my usual secular show—but with a difference.

Don asked me to include all of my Christian testimony.

At first I felt reluctant to do this. Then, as I understood what he was trying to do, it became intriguing. You see, Don sponsored this performance as a means of entertaining some of the church members, and gradually leading them into a discussion of tithing.

It's a very unorthodox method, I guess, but finally I decided to go along with it. I really socked it to them. Not only did I do my usual show, but this time we included some of my testimony, the plan of salvation, plus my witness regarding tithing. "You simply can't out-bless God," I told them.

Eventually their church surpassed their tithing goal by ten thousand dollars—and I was glad I'd helped. Another reason we were glad we accepted the booking is that Don Sanders and some other men from his church came down to Miami to study some of our church programs—the bus ministry and so on.

The service seemed to touch their hearts.

"Your church has something we just don't have," Don told us. Bob and I are praying for the Spirit of God to set fire to the hearts of that wonderful Syracuse congregation.

Early in December, Northwest Baptist held a dinner to honor the deacons. They asked me to sing and give my testimony, and it thrilled my heart to do this on our very first such dinner—to take part in honoring my husband, along with the others.

Three months earlier, when Bob had been installed in that office, I cut a rose from our garden and handed it to him with the following poem:

> A rose for my deacon, to remind you that
> "The Rose of Sharon" was cut off for you!
> And through Christ's example you can grow in

grace and knowledge,
And let your light shine to all like a beacon!
A deacon's wife,
ANITA
September 15, 1973


And then, miraculously, once again the world turned toward Christmas. Despite the struggles and strains in our
household, beyond our preoccupations with details of our
individual lives (someone once said the trouble with life is,
it's so *daily!*), even despite the kids' bouts with viruses, suddenly we could each hear something of the angels' songs.

God gave us a special, special Christmas time. I asked Bob
not to book us at all during the holidays, except for the
church cantata and for one football game on December 30.
Instead, we saved those precious holidays for our friends and
family.

This was the first time my dad and his wife, Jewel, and
later my brother, Sonny, visited in our home for Christmas.
I wanted everything to be perfect.

We planned a party for the Friday evening Dad and Jewel
were to arrive. We invited our church staff, some of the
Miami Dolphins and their wives, show-business friends, people from every walk of life. We wanted Dad and Jewel to
know some of the people in our lives—and a most interesting
group it was, too.

Externally, at the last moment things began going wrong.
We planned to have the party in our courtyard, and had
rented round tables to set out. The day before, the heavens
opened up; rain poured down all day. Teddy and I prayed
it wouldn't rain for the party, and it didn't—but it turned
freezing cold, instead.

Then Dad and Jewel's plane got delayed. By the time they arrived, there were only thirty minutes before party time. I wore my long, red Christmas dress to meet them at the airport.

This is the year the Lord has tried to teach me not to panic. Day-by-day He tells me—in every way imaginable—"Anita, you can panic if you want to—or you can trust Me." I'm trying to learn to trust.

That evening, as I fought traffic headed toward the airport, I decided to let God handle the situation. Suddenly I thought back to an episode in Atlanta a couple of weeks earlier. Bob and I were autographing books at Rich's Department Store, and everybody in the long line seemed to have armloads of books to be signed.

Faith Brunson, manager of the Book Department and an officer of the American Booksellers Association, noticed me eyeing all those books. I just praised the Lord, however, smiled and kept on signing my name. Later Faith commented, "I don't know what has happened to you, but you sure are different."

"Oh, boy!" I said silently agreeing that tribulation worketh patience. Maybe God *is* making me more patient—helping me to trust.

Greeting Dad and Jewel at the airport, I immediately noticed their concern at the late hour. "Don't worry," I reassured them. "You just go up to the guest apartment, shower, freshen up, then come down when you wish. There's all the time in the world."

And there was. As for the freezing weather, I just let God handle that detail, too. "Father, please let each guest really feel the Presence of the Lord tonight, and experience His love. Please bless us with the warmth of Your Presence."

Later I got rather tickled as one guest after another would mention the "warmth" of the gathering, or the "warm-hearted" atmosphere.

Bob gave our family a beautiful electric organ for Christmas. That evening Chuck Bird, my arranger-conductor, played the new instrument and I sang "Silent Night, Holy Night." As always, that simple song worked its own magic in our hearts.

On the Sunday night before Christmas, our family gathered at church for the annual Christmas cantata. I sang a solo, but Bob narrated the entire cantata—and did a great job. Then I gave a few words of testimony and sang "Silent Night." Brother Bill Chapman closed with a prayer and an invitation.

God gave us so many sweet moments during those days. Bob and Bobby, Daddy and Charlie Morgan, all heading out to see a Miami Dolphins football game . . . my father playing granddad to four excited kids on Christmas morning . . . our family attending church together . . . Christmas dinner, very traditional and replete with roast suckling pig and all the trimmings, which I cooked . . . Bob's parents, Farmor and Farfar, adding their Swedish *Jul* cheeriness to our household. . . .

Dad and Jewel visited us for five wonderful days. Meanwhile Sonny stayed home to care for their fine herd of beautiful Black Angus cattle.

When they returned to Oklahoma, Sonny flew down for the rest of the holidays. And then, for the first time, I really got to know my brother. I like him. He's great, and God was supergood to give Sonny to us for Christmas.

In so many ways, we'd had a tough year. But in so many other ways, God had blessed us beyond anything we've ever known.

Those days fairly sparkled. Everything sang of Christmas: four happy children; our tree, tipping the ceiling, heavy with old ornaments; the scent of evergreens; sounds of laughter and carols; friends and relatives; music from our new organ; the holiday foods I cooked. . . .

Favorite things. An old song welled up in me:

> Joy to the world! The Lord has come!
> Let earth receive her King!

# 12

# Strengthen Thy Brethren

The Apostle Peter is someone I really identify with.

Good old Peter—impulsive, impetuous, walking on the water, and sinking like a stone—oh, how I recognize his type!

But Peter passionately loved his Lord, and Jesus loved him. Luke 22:31, 32 describes this in a beautiful way:

> And the Lord said, Simon, Simon, behold, Satan hath desired to have you, that he may sift you as wheat:
>
> But I have prayed for thee, that thy faith fail not: and when thou art converted, strengthen thy brethren.

Do those words speak to you as they do to me?

Can you imagine our Lord anxious for *your* soul, fearful for Satan's power over *you?*

Can you see Jesus Himself pray for you . . . believe in your conversion . . . then admonish you to strengthen your brothers?

The very thought of how much Jesus cares, thrills my heart. Many times these past months Satan desired to have me, and would have "sifted me as wheat." That's when we need to put on the whole armor of God, as Paul teaches us in Ephesians 6:11–20, so as to withstand the assaults of the devil.

Jesus is teaching me that when I strengthen my brother I also strengthen myself. When any part of the body of Christ suffers, all suffer. Therefore the process of trying to strengthen another—my neighbor, my child, a stranger—done for Christ's sake, will bless me (the giver) as well.

I'm looking at an entry in my diary where I wrote, "Praise God! He's full of surprises!" That day I had learned all over again that no matter how down or discouraged you get, or how out of fellowship, God always will give you a way out. He always gives you a chance to come back to Him.

I'd suffered a spiritual setback, what seemed a severe rejection, and in my discouragement decided I'd quit teaching my Sunday-school class. I brought it up at teachers' meeting that Wednesday night, and Brother Joe Vellines gave me a Scripture: "If we suffer, we shall also reign with him" (2 Timothy 2:12).

My colleagues considered what I said, then carefully gave their reactions. It boiled down to their need for teachers. Toni and Edsel Gainey and Charlie Porter reminded me that we don't have enough teachers in our rapidly growing church. They said that even if you consider you're doing much less than an ideal job, there's simply nobody else to take over.

There was just one thing to do, of course—yield the situation to Jesus. This I did.

The following Sunday God sent me a surprise package— a little girl named Alex Sheenan, who sometimes accompanied one of our regular girls to Sunday school on the Judah bus route. That day our lesson concerned three kinds of lostness: to be lost from safety; lost from usefulness; and lost from fellowship.

After each of these points, I asked the girls to join hands and I led them in prayer. Then I asked if there were anyone present who was lost in that particular way. When I queried them about being lost from safety, little Alex raised her hand.

After class, I talked with Alex and she asked Jesus to come into her heart. She cried as she prayed on her knees the sinner's prayer, and when I put my arms around her she thanked me for caring about her. That was the day I went home and wrote that exuberant entry in my diary.

That same week, I began my visitation program. I try to visit each of my eleven-year-olds in her home at least once a year, and to stay in regular contact by telephone the rest of the time. Now it was time to begin visiting.

When you embark on church visitation, it can really open your eyes. You learn many, many things about the world Jesus loved and instructed us to go into.

Our church, a tremendously soul-winning church, believes in visiting. Tuesdays are ladies' visitation days, and certain sisters assign themselves hours to come to our sanctuary and pray and then go forth into the community to witness. Those of us who visit, go out in pairs. While one speaks, the other silently prays. We have learned that this technique really works well for the Lord.

Jody Dunton agreed to go with me on that fresh January morning. I had telephoned ahead and knew just which homes to visit, and in what order. There weren't enough cars to go around, so Jody took another gal visiting in her car and Diane Elam went with me. Jody and I were to meet back at the church at twelve noon, have lunch, and then continue visiting for the rest of the day.

One of my girls had not come to Sunday school in a while, and when I phoned her home, her mother told me she was going to The Seed on Sundays and couldn't come to church. I felt so shocked and stunned. The Seed is a local organization which helps drug addicts who want to kick the problem. Here was my little eleven-year-old, battling for her spiritual life as she painfully withdrew from the drug scene.

Eleven years old! The Seed does tremendous work, but it is not a Christian organization. I got so depressed, thinking about my little student, and how I wished I had the time and means and fortitude to establish a Christian drug-fighting organization here in Miami.

That episode alone would have been enough to convince me that the Lord needs soldiers to fight for our children, to lead them to the safety of Jesus before the pushers get them.

Evil influences come into a child's life very early these days. No longer can you even assume they are safe at school. If eleven-year-olds succumb to peer-group pressures and begin experimenting with drugs, obviously we've got to start even earlier than that to win them to Christ.

It scares me.

Almost every kid I visited, I soon realized, had adult-sized burdens to bear. Little Donna Sidelinker, for example, had just had a traumatic experience. A week earlier, while bike riding with a friend, a car struck the other girl. The child died before Donna's eyes.

"Donna—child or adult—none of us knows when we might go to be with Jesus," I told her. "We must be ready. Was your friend a Christian?"

"Oh, yes," she assured me.

"Are you?" Donna wrinkled her little brow while she tried to decide the answer to that one. She wasn't sure.

"Donna, do you want to have a spiritual birthday? Would you like to know there was a time and a place where you invited Jesus to come into your heart to live forever?"

She knew the answer to that. Then and there, little Donna Sidelinker turned her young life over to Jesus. Praise God, Diane Elam and I had the joy of helping that little one trust the Lord.

God had other, even more sobering experiences ahead for Jody Dunton and me as we continued visiting. There was Alex Sheenan, for example, the girl who had trusted Jesus just the other day. I was eager to visit her home. We needed to talk about baptism for Alex.

Home turned out to be a shabby upstairs flat in a run-down section of Miami Beach. Alex answered our knock promptly. Jody and I walked in to a shocking situation.

Frank Gleman, the child's grandfather and legal guardian, spent most of his time in bed. We'd had no idea he was seriously ill; now we learned that cancer had cost him a lung, a kidney, several ribs, and a leg.

He suffered much pain, despite heavy medication. We learned that Frank had been given custody of Alex when she was just six months old. He loved the child dearly.

Frank, only weeks before, at Christmas time, had lost his wife. His doctors considered him too seriously ill to attend her funeral. Now he was all alone, except for Alex, who had taken over the cooking and housekeeping. Our hearts went out to this valiant man.

I sat right down on Frank's bed and talked to him, sharing Alex's recent experience with the Lord. He seemed delighted and relieved to hear about it. Soon he and I were talking about *him*—and I asked if there had been a time and a place when he received Jesus Christ as his Lord and Saviour.

Frank said he didn't know what he would have done all these years during his illness and trying to raise Sandy (his pet name for Alex), if he hadn't had faith in God. He talked quite a while and I realized he believed in God but had never *personally* received Christ into his heart and life. I poured my heart out to Frank Gleman, knowing his situation to be critical. We read Romans 9:10, 11, and John 3:1–21. I shared Teddy's trinity with him, then Jody, Alex, Frank and I held hands and prayed and Frank Gleman came to the Lord!

Talk about Jesus' instruction to "strengthen thy brethren"! It shook me and humbled me—as well as strengthened me—to realize how God had used me *twice in one day* to lead a precious soul to Him.

Jody and I rushed back to church to get Frank a Bible and some tracts on baptism. We rejoiced all the way, and rejoiced even more as we shared God's goodness with the faithful friends who prayed for us as we visited.

God used Frank Gleman to bless our entire congregation. Jody and I became quite involved and burdened for him and Alex in all areas of their lives, and especially on the matter of their baptism.

Now if ever a man had any excuse to forego baptism, it was Frank. He lives with severe pain. An amputee, he seldom even feels like sitting in his wheelchair. He remains confined to bed for longer and longer hours with each week that passes.

Nevertheless, Frank wanted to be baptized. I telephoned the Veterans Administration Hospital for permission, and his doctors went into a huddle. Soon they rang back, to give their approval. Baptism might be difficult for Frank, since two men would have to lift him into the pool, but it could be done—if he could find a day sufficiently free of pain for him to stand the experience.

Frank stood firm in his desire. We scheduled his baptism —no easy task, since we needed quite a bit of coordination for the procedure—but then had to call it off, because he was racked with pain. Undaunted, Frank simply rescheduled the ceremony. His beloved Alex intended to be baptized at the same time. Jody and I could hardly tell which mattered more to him—her baptism, or his own.

The next time we went to get Frank, to prepare him for Sunday evening church, again we found him pain-filled. Charlie Walker and another of the deacons from the church, Bill Luman, had accompanied me, planning to lift Frank down the stairs and into the station wagon.

"Let's pray for Frank," Charlie said quietly.

"Yes. Let's join hands, too," I suggested. "And let's . . . let's just put our other hand on Frank. . . ."

I remembered how often Jesus reached out and touched those He would heal. Somehow I just yearned to touch Frank, to let him feel the love of Christ in a tangible way. So that's just what we did.

About five minutes later, Frank's pain had subsided.

So Charlie and Bill joined in cleaning the kitchen while Alex dressed for church. Elated, I began to sing at the top of my voice while, unknown to me, some little kids started gathering downstairs.

Charlie Walker made a trip downstairs to take out the trash and saw the kids congregated below. "Know who that is?" he asked them. "That's Anita Bryant singing."

They didn't believe him, so Charlie yelled up at the kitchen window for me to sing "The Florida Sunshine Tree" song. I sang it, and the kids believed!

At church, Ray and Linda Parker (who worked on the

Baptismal Committee and on the bus ministry for many years and have since gone to work with Wycliffe Bible translators) gathered around Frank's wheelchair and prayed for him, before services began. We also learned that Alex had a terrible fear of water, so we prayed for God to deliver her from that fear.

Their baptism touched my heart and inspired me as few things ever have done. It blessed the entire church to see this man carried into the water, helpless, yet obedient to his Lord.

Brother Bill looked tall and solemn as he performed the ceremony. Our sanctuary was hushed as the brethren witnessed this special moment.

"I prophesy that someday this man will have a perfect body," Brother Bill said with a grin on his face.

*Amen!*

I'm just hitting the high spots. Time after time God has shown me that when we do try to strengthen our brother, *we* end up with extra blessings of our own.

There was a Time of Renewal, for example.

That blessed day grew out of an invitation extended to me through Marabel Morgan from Evelyn Galvin of the Miami Shores Presbyterian Church who had a concern for the young women in her church and wanted to inspire them. This time, instead of just singing and testifying, I yearned to do something more—but I didn't know exactly what.

Immediately I consulted with Teddy Heard, of course. Teddy simply overflowed with creative ideas. And as we talked, it came to me: This would be an ideal occasion for Teddy's small-group experiences.

The whole thing grew by leaps and bounds. I persuaded Teddy to come to Miami to guide the project. Suddenly, instead of confining itself to the Presbyterians, a Time of Renewal had spread by word of mouth and by invitation until several hundred women from top denominations like the Miami Shores Community Church, and many others, had registered for what turned out to be one of the most exciting times of my life.

Teddy trained, instructed, and inspired the small-group leaders—gals like Marabel Morgan, Anne Huffman, Peggy Chapman, Becky Barrett, Fredda Walker, Kathy Miller, Nancy Kolen. Although most of these came from Northwest Baptist Church, there were others from all denominations. "You are facilitators," she told them. "There's even greater resource within a group gathered in Jesus' Name than there is in just one person."

Teddy and I really didn't know what our testimony would be. Both of us felt burdened as to how to approach people from so many different denominations and bring them to a point of decision.

We knew the small-group concept would work. But the multidenominational congregation was something *way* out of my experience. I knew there were Jewish women, for example, in the groups.

As Teddy and I prayed beforehand, the Lord burdened me not to be ashamed of the Gospel—God forbid!—but that I must present it in such a way that any of them might be drawn magnetically to the love of God. I yearned to bring these women to a decision point in their lives.

I used the first chapter of the Gospel of John, which describes Jesus as the light of the world, and goes on to tell that "as many as received him, to them gave he power to become the sons of God . . ." (John 1:12). I sang and gave my testimony for over an hour, then I introduced Teddy, quoting Daniel 12:3. Then Teddy spoke and shared her three circles.

What a life-changing day! Women were packed and stacked into the main sanctuary and then gathered in little groups—upstairs, downstairs, outside—in every possible space, listening attentively.

Everyone related. Denominational differences were put aside. The love of God filled that room, uplifted, and inspired each one of us. The love of God touched those little groups. We broke for lunch and then had a final meeting together. Many women received Christ and many rededicated their lives to Him that day.

A Time of Renewal evolved into a landmark experience in my own Christian life, and I heard many another woman make the same statement. We learned to speak the truth in love. We learned creative sharing—the give and take of Christian experience—the ways we can encourage fellow strugglers.

"Everyone is at a different place on the Christian road," Teddy explained. "We gain by giving of what the Lord has given us.

"I used to think the Christian life was living above the jungle," she told us. "Now I know it's living *in* the jungle."

Teddy never swerved away from opportunities to head into life, no matter where they took her. Her example taught me so much for, brilliant as she was with words and thoughts, her life itself glowed with the power of God's love.

Often I ponder God's timing, His perfect timetable for all things. A Time of Renewal stands out as a fantastic example of this.

It's as though He sent Teddy to us to show women in my community the power of concerted Christian action. For me, it became a training course in leadership. A Time of Renewal demonstrated practical Christian renewal at work—spontaneous and unrehearsed—guided by God's Holy Spirit.

"I know you don't want to hear this," Teddy began when the long day was over and at last we could compare notes, "But Anita, I think God gave me a glimpse of your mission.

"Today we really had a foretaste of what He intends for you, I feel sure.

"If you are obedient, I believe Jesus will teach you not only to lead individuals, but groups."

She was right! I didn't want to hear it.

That day, exhilarated beyond measure, I bubbled over with joy and excitement about wonderful joint projects Teddy and I might undertake in years to come.

I didn't dream, of course, that there would be no more years on this earth for Teddy and me—but only a few months.

Now I look back in wonder and awe to realize how creatively God utilized all the time Teddy and I were to have. Not only was she my friend, my sister, but my Christian instructress as well.

How often—how *very* often—God led Teddy to strengthen me!

# Anita

## 13
## "I Scarce Can Take It In. . . ."

Precious in the sight of the Lord is the death of his saints.

Psalms 116:15

Neither Teddy nor I knew much about death or dying. Oh, we discussed these subjects as we discussed everything else under the sun—with curiosity, wonder, and interest. Intellectually, we knew the Christian attitude toward physical death. Experientially, it was an unknown quantity.

And so, when Teddy entered the hospital for surgery—major surgery, it's true, but very ordinary in nature—we reacted as we did to everything else. We discussed it, prayed about it, asked for God's guidance, affirmed one another, and kidded about it.

Danger? That never occurred to either of us. We were so close, so empathetic and sisterly—surely I'd know if anything went wrong. And anyhow, why worry? If Teddy had taught me anything at all, she taught me that.

Two days following surgery, I felt Teddy might feel up to talking to me. I had a million things to tell her, and couldn't wait to hear her voice. Imagine my consternation, therefore, when I learned she had complications. Further surgery was needed.

From that day forward, my beloved friend endured one crisis after another. Despite my determination to operate by faith, not fear, her condition worsened so inexorably that I found it increasingly difficult to believe God would provide a miracle.

Everyone was praying for a miracle, of course. People all over America—Christians and non-Christians, people from all walks of life—prayed without ceasing for God to spare Teddy Heard. At thirty-nine, this woman already had influenced many, many lives. More people loved her than most of us ever will know.

How well I knew Teddy's attitudes toward trouble! She believed in facing life squarely, dealing with facts rather than fears, and turning every aspect of one's life over to God's loving care. She and Wyatt practiced this philosophy with their four youngsters: Larry, fifteen; Teddy, thirteen; Susannah, eleven, and Denman, seven. The children kept faithful prayer vigils for their mother. Once or twice when I telephoned to learn of her condition, little Teddy informed me, "Mama almost died last night, but God pulled her through again."

Our precious Teddy remained in Intensive Care for nearly four weeks as some of the world's finest specialists battled to save her life. Alarmed, her friends could do little more than stand by and pray as her bodily functions began to fail.

Marabel Morgan and I dogmatically believed that Jesus Christ would restore Teddy Heard to perfect health. So much so that I decided not to fly to Houston. Daily and even hourly we prayed, never doubting, and the worse the news became, the more we insisted that God would be glorified through the miracle of healing He was creating. God had told me she would be healed and become an even brighter beacon for His glory.

That was true. The healing, however, was not within Teddy's body; it took place in the Body of Christ, within those believers who needed to see God in all His magnificence. Even as some of us prayed wholeheartedly and believed with all our strength, and even had a peace about it, we wished to resist God's answer when it arrived.

Why, God, *why?*

Oh, God, I don't want to pray, "Thy will be done. . . ."

Anita Bryant was one who until virtually the last hour confidently believed God would answer those prayers—and answer them her way. My faith would not be moved. I dared not jeopardize Teddy's safety by allowing that faith to waver by so much as the blink of an eye.

And then came that final Sunday afternoon, and one of the usual telephone conversations with Dow Heard—Teddy's brother-in-law—from the hospital in Houston.

For the first time, Dow sounded bleak. It made me want to panic. As he recited the facts in his calm, smooth voice, explaining his fading hopes, I felt anger rise in me.

"No, Dow, we must trust God for a miracle," I began.

"We have," he said quietly. "And she has suffered terribly. They can't give her anything at all for the pain. Her body has been assaulted by everything imaginable. Machines keep her alive. Her strength is gone, yet whenever she is conscious she praises God. Her voice is just a whisper. It can't be much longer, Anita."

"No, Dow, *no.*" I could not accept what he was saying.

"We can't do anything at all for Teddy that is not being done," he continued. "It's Wyatt who needs us most. Please pray he'll be able to relinquish her completely to the Lord."

I could hardly answer. My mind swirled around crazily, trying to reject Dow's words. There must be some other answer, some other way to pray. . . .

Relinquish her? No. I could not, would not, pray that.

Bob couldn't do much with me. To my shocked horror, he agreed with Dow. "Does it occur to you that you may be blocking the will of God through your prayers?" he asked.

"Can you honestly pray that God's will be done? Or do you keep demanding that *your* will be done?" I almost hated him for saying that.

"Anita, please phone Brother Bill and let him counsel you," Bob gently suggested. "Don't listen to me. Let our pastor guide your thinking. These next days will be critical for Teddy. Let's find out how to pray for her in God's will. Let's align ourselves with His purposes."

Of course Bob was right. I dialed Brother Bill's number with fear and trembling. I felt great forebodings by now, and dreaded what he might say.

"Anita, we must trust God totally with our most treasured people," he told me. "Do you truly believe God loves Teddy and wants only her perfect happiness?"

"Of course!" I burst out. "That's why I have the boldness to claim the victory for her. I *know* God could not want to take a thirty-nine-year-old woman away from those who love her and need her. I can't see any sense at all in that!"

"Anita, do you really believe Romans 8:28?"

"Yes-s-s."

"Then can you trust God to work things together for good?"

"Certainly," I whispered, my stomach by now in knots.

"Then let's pray we can just let her go and let God do what He will. Let's relinquish Teddy to the Lord."

That terrible word again. Brother Bill prayed. When I left the telephone, I felt that the light had gone out in my world.

I could find no peace anywhere. There was no use trying to pray, because turmoil possessed me. I couldn't read or talk or think. At last I walked outside and stared into the calm, gray waters of Biscayne Bay.

Why? Where was the sense in it? . . . How could a loving God . . . ?

Something interrupted my silent, angry questions.

Suddenly, quite abruptly, a question cut through my conscious thoughts: *Do you love her more than Me?* I stood there, motionless, waiting for something.

*Do you love her? More than Me?* The thought persisted. I could not answer. The question returned, more urgent this time than before: *Anita, do you love her more than Me?*

Something in me broke. "No, Lord," I whispered at last. "No. No one, Lord, more than You."

*Then trust Me,* He said, and repeated it twice again. *Trust Me. Trust Me.* And then something directed my feet toward the house, up the stairs, into the den where the bookshelves were. Instinctively I headed straight for a certain book— *Beyond Our Selves*—by Catherine Marshall. Teddy's sister, Rhetta McAlister, had mentioned a week before how it had ministered to her needs.

Hurriedly I flipped the pages, searching, scanning—and then I found it, a passage concerning the prayer of relinquishment. I knew I must read it then and there, but I could not. My eyes would not focus.

I hurried downstairs and gathered my family around me, needing comfort, needing their help. I thrust the book into

Bob's hands and ordered him to read to us about *relinquish-ment*—hateful word!—while I clung to my children's hands, hung my head, and wept.

I was beginning to accept the facts, and they were unbeara-ble. I felt turmoil, shock, unbelief, fear—and I could not hear the words Bob read.

Suddenly I remembered something Wyatt had said some days before—something about being willing to be willing. I knew I had to come to that place, but I was not ready.

We attended training union that evening. As we drove across the causeway and toward the church we looked straight into the sinking sun—so bright, so brilliant. It made me think of Teddy. Why, God? Why?

At church I was in shock, just going through the motions. Reality approached, however, despite everything I could do. *Lord, speak to me in this service. Tell me You're not going to take her. . . .*

But my faith, my dogmatic faith, was gone. I had prayed without ceasing, yet it was gone. . . .

Brother Bill preached about women—Lot's wife, Job's wife—all those wretched women. Then he said that Mary of Bethany had provided the finest testimony in all the Bible about what your relationship to Jesus can be. She witnessed through offering an alabaster box full of ointment, and in worship anointing the head of Jesus as a memorial to His burial.

Instantly I knew. He's talking about Teddy!

Her life was like an alabaster box. She poured her life out on mankind, in worship of the Lord Jesus Christ. It was as though Jesus were saying of Teddy, "She hath done what she could."

The more Brother Bill talked the more it seemed to me I

was hearing Teddy's memorial service preached—that God was telling me He intended to take her.

I couldn't bear it, it was so horrible.

I felt absolutely frozen, crouched in our pew listening to that nightmarish sermon, totally frozen except for the tears that rushed down my cheeks.

The burden bent me over. It was there, but I could not give it to God. He had told me bad news and I knew it, but I could not accept it.

The invitation came, but I could not go forward. I would settle this thing alone with God when I got home. But then He gave just one more invitation, and I stumbled forward. I had to have peace.

"She's Yours . . . Your will be done," I sobbed. Then, after prayer, peace came over me. I could hear and accept Brother Bill's comment that Teddy would say, "If God can get more glory out of taking me, I want to go." I knew that was true.

I made many phone calls asking people to pray for Teddy, to beg God for a miracle. When I called Charlotte Topping, I felt funny about it for a moment. Charlotte's husband lived so near the edge of death, after all; I was sorry to bring up the subject. However, her response surprised me.

"Oh, Anita, to go and be with Jesus! How wonderful that would be!" she said, her voice wistful. It was as if Charlotte saw it all in a whole different light.

I felt a little rebuked, as I had the day before when Bobby, clasping my hand, asked, "Mommie, why are you crying? Black people celebrate when someone dies!"

It was Monday, and Chuck Bird came over to rehearse me for our engagement at Stetson University that Wednesday. The school, located in DeLand, Florida, had invited me to speak at Women's Emphasis Week and give my Christian testimony in word and song. This was our only opportunity to rehearse.

Just as we began, the phone rang. It was Dow Heard in Houston.

"Anita, she can't make it. She may go tonight . . . maybe hang on a few days longer."

"I know, Dow. The Lord told me yesterday."

Dow was surprised. This was a complete turnaround on my part. Gone was that dogmatic, implacable faith he was expecting. He must have felt unnerved.

"Anita . . . I don't like to do this, but there's no one else. I must ask you if you would . . . sing . . . if. . . ."

"Of course, Dow. You know we'll be there. Of course I'll sing." I explained our schedule was full that week, but surely God would work things out. Then I prayed for Dow, asking God to give him strength and fortitude.

After the phone call, I wept. Then we had to rehearse. That took such discipline, and Chuck hated to put me through it. "I don't understand any of it, Chuck, but I know God has a purpose in all this," I told him.

That night at 10:30 Wyatt telephoned us from the hospital. He sounded unutterably weary. He had remained at Teddy's side for long days and nights, watching every little flicker of change in her condition.

"It's God's business. Whatever He wants to do is all right," Wyatt said, his voice breaking. "I just praise Him."

Afterwards I fled to the music room, sank to my knees, and prayed and wept for more than an hour. Sometime during that period Teddy went to be with Jesus.

It was after one A.M. when the phone rang again, waking us from deep sleep. "Anita, this is Brother Ken Chafin,

Teddy's pastor. She passed away at about 11:30."

Quickly we made arrangements. Somehow we'd attend Teddy's services. The Lord would have to get us to DeLand on that same evening, or He'd have to instruct us to cancel that booking.

The moment I placed the telephone on the receiver I began to cry—deep, guttural, tearing, gutsy weeping. Bob took me into his arms and silently rocked me to and fro, rocked me as you'd hold a baby, tears rolling down his cheeks.

It was very tender and very devastating.

At last, when it all had come out, I got on my knees beside the bed. "Can you pray for me?" I asked him.

It was over. I had come to the end of expressing my grief. There were no tears, no words, no prayers left.

Bob prayed in a strong, quiet voice—prayed for me, for Wyatt, for the Heard children, for everybody who hurt. And then I just fell back, spent, and said a rather strange thing: "I scarce can take it in," I murmured.

"Come to bed," Bob ordered. I obeyed him.

At four A.M. I woke up suddenly and sat straight up in bed. The thought came to me strongly, ". . . I scarce can take it in."

What did that mean? Suddenly I realized the source of those words. They are part of the third lyric of "How Great Thou Art." I didn't know the rest of the words, because I never sang that verse—always just the first and second stanzas of the song.

I rushed down to the music room. I couldn't wait to learn those lyrics, because I knew they were for Teddy's family. At last in my office I found what I hunted:

And when I think that God, His Son not sparing,

Sent him to die, I scarce can take it in;

That on the cross, my burden gladly bearing,

He bled and died to take away my sin.*

I hardly believed my eyes. Here was the very heart of the Gospel, in a verse I never sang. Then and there I vowed never to omit that verse again.

Charlotte Topping made a prediction: "You've got to be strong. You must not cry," she told me.

Marabel Morgan phoned to promise they'd pray for me. "I know she'll have a glorious coronation ceremony, and the Lord will anoint you in a special way," she said.

Later Stephanie Noonan, the beautiful wife of former Miami Dolphin Carl Noonan, called to say, "I just read Ephesians 1:10. Teddy was taken as an early gift." I wrote that Scripture down to share with Wyatt and the rest of the family.

Bob called our good friends at Revell to give them the sad news of Teddy's passing. Teddy's first book titled *Love Power* was to be published this year. They would go ahead as planned with the book.

Judge Heard, who for many days sent regular bulletins reporting his wife's condition, sent one final message to their numerous friends:

At approximately eleven P.M. on March 4, 1974, Mrs. Wyatt H. Heard met her Savior face to face. Jesus Christ, who died on the cross for her as for us all, received her into His

ever-loving arms. Funeral services will be held at 11:00 A.M.
at South Main Baptist Church, Houston, Texas, Wednesday,
March 6, 1974.

WYATT H. HEARD

Psalms 148:1–4          Psalms 149:4          Psalms 150:6

As we traveled toward Houston I read a small book entitled *The Sacred Spot,* written by Ted Lewis Moody, Teddy's
mother. In that joyous and inspiring book, I discovered the
Bible verse which was Teddy's special heritage from her
grandmother and her mother—and which she passed on to
her four children, in turn.

> Don't worry over anything whatever; tell God every detail
> of your needs in earnest and thankful prayer, and the peace
> of God, which transcends human understanding, will keep
> constant guard over your hearts and minds as they rest in
> Christ Jesus.

*See* Philippians 4:6, 7

I had to smile. Both sentimental and practical, Teddy had
that verse inscribed on a special key ring for me. "That way
you'll read it every time you use your car keys," she said.

Mrs. Denman Moody, Teddy's angel mother, always calls
her oldest daughter's funeral services her "graduation exercise."

Everything about the occasion spelled out victory. If ever
I saw a convincing demonstration of victory over death, I
was to see it time and again in the attitudes of family and
friends, and in the triumphant Christian church services
which honored Teddy.

I wore a simple white silk suit with my gold fishhook. Teddy would have liked it, and she would have been glad to hear me say to Dan Yeary that for me this was Easter. Three days earlier, I had descended into death and anguish of the spirit; today, miraculously, with Teddy Heard I experienced a resurrection with Christ. Joanne Heard, Teddy's sister-in-law, came over to me and said, "I'm praying for you and expect to see the anointed oil of the Holy Spirit just dripping off of you." At the time I thought that was an odd thing to say, until a week later Marabel and Charlie Morgan, as I told them of the incident, shared with me this Scripture: "To appoint unto them that mourn in Zion, to give unto them beauty for ashes, the oil of joy for mourning . . ." (Isaiah 61:3).

The huge Baptist church in downtown Houston overflowed with celebrants as some 5,200 friends paid tribute to a radiant and good young woman. Never could I forget the joyous, worshipful atmosphere we shared that day. I hear the organ music: "On Christ the Solid Rock I Stand"; "How Firm a Foundation"; and then—sweetly—"Jesus Loves Me."

I see the faces of her loved ones, not sorrowful, but tranquil and full of trust. I hear the voice of her beloved childhood pastor, Dr. Charles King, reading favorite verses from God's magnificent Word. And then Dr. E. H. Westmoreland's heartrending prayer, and the gentle words of the Reverend Kenneth Chafin, her pastor at the South Main Baptist Church, describing Teddy's life in such loving terms.

Throughout the entire service, you could feel the Presence of our living Lord. He stayed close beside each one of us, loving us, rejoicing with us, during the most indescribably beautiful hour I ever experienced.

Once when I glanced up it was as if I could see Teddy, all excited and aglow, looking into the face of Jesus. I saw her joy, and I felt it, too.

Oh, God, this is what it's like for Teddy to be in Your Presence right now, I thought.

I felt so joyful I wanted to shout aloud—or do a David dance! I truly experienced what God has in store for each of us: the promise of the unspeakable joy which comes from living in His Presence forever!

This is what I told all those wonderful people who loved Teddy as I did: "Teddy was my sister—not my blood sister —but by a stronger bond: the blood of Jesus Christ. How I loved her! And how I love her still, and Wyatt, and the children, and the family. I once introduced her, feeling that Daniel 12:3 perfectly described her. Then before coming here I read the verse above that and I'd like to share it with you this morning. Verse two in The Living Bible reads, 'And many of those whose bodies lie dead and buried will rise up, some to everlasting life and some to shame and everlasting contempt.' And here is verse three, which is Teddy: 'And those who are wise—the people of God—shall shine as brightly as the sun's brilliance, and those who turn many to righteousness will glitter like stars forever.'"

God helped me sing as I never sang before. "How Great Thou Art" burst forth, and each member of that huge, united family which bore and reared and loved Teddy looked into my face as I sang it. I saw the love of Jesus in every single countenance, a vivid scene forever etched on my mind. I knew and understood the love that made Teddy, Teddy.

Then it was done. We joined voices in one magnificent hymn "How Firm a Foundation." That is a hymn for Christians to live by!

How firm a foundation, ye saints of the Lord,
Is laid for your faith in His excellent Word!
What more can He say than to you He hath said,
To you who for refuge to Jesus have fled?

Fear not, I am with thee; O be not dismayed!
For I am thy God, I will still give thee aid;
I'll strengthen thee, help thee, and cause thee to stand,
Upheld by My gracious, omnipotent hand.

When through the deep waters I call thee to go,
The rivers of sorrow shall not overflow;
For I will be with thee thy trials to bless,
And sanctify to thee thy deepest distress.

When through fiery trials thy pathway shall lie,
My grace, all-sufficient, shall be thy supply;
The flame shall not hurt thee; I only design
Thy dross to consume, and thy gold to refine.

The soul that on Jesus hath leaned for repose
I will not, I will not desert to his foes:
That soul, though all hell should endeavor to shake,
I'll never, no, never, no, never forsake.


On our way to the airport I could put my head on Bob's
shoulder and for the first time, we could cry together. Bob
had been honored to be one of the pallbearers. It was a first
for him. We wept from full hearts and out of gladness. We
shed tears of thankfulness for our beautiful friend and the
lives she touched.

God provided a charter flight—a Lear jet—which carried
us to DeLand for the engagement at Stetson University. We
marveled at the generosity of Teddy's friend, Janie Beeler,

who saw that we were transported, in excellent time, and praised God for meeting our need.

That very morning we still didn't know how we would get to DeLand, Florida, in time. We came to Houston on faith, for all commercial flights arrived too late for the DeLand performance that evening. Bob was panicky, so I insisted that Bob, Virginia Berkeley, and I hold hands and pray that God would provide our transportation and even get us there in time for rehearsal. (We had spent the night with Dr. and Mrs. Ralph Berkeley, close friends of Wyatt and Teddy, and it was Virginia Berkeley who mentioned our desperate transportation needs to Janie Beeler in the South Main Baptist Church parking lot right before the funeral service.) Janie made calls to her husband, Dick, president of Jetro Construction Company, and others, thus getting the ball rolling. As the services ended, we received the good news and we all praised the Lord that He not only answers prayers but He answers them *first class!*

Chuck and Hope Bird met us at the airport. My favorite conductor-arranger has worked with us for ten wonderful and hectic years, and he knows me pretty well. Two days earlier he had seen me in defeat; now, through the power of God, I radiated joy and health. Chuck marveled at the things we told him.

Stetson University is a Baptist school, and I enjoyed appearing there that evening. I shared with Dean Etta Turner and the students everything God did for us that day—told about Teddy, her death and resurrection to eternal life with Jesus, told of the faith and triumph evidenced by thousands of Christians who attended her "graduation" that morning.

I sang and testified—and wept. The Lord Jesus washed out my eyes, but those blessed students didn't seem to mind.

Later they crowded back towards the reception, eager to speak, and many shared how they had rededicated their lives to Jesus that evening.

Oh, Teddy, that's for you, I thought.

Teddy would have loved it. Bob and I had a perfect ending to a glorious day. We went to bed exhausted and tear-stained, but radiant and filled with praise.

# 14

# Great and Mighty Things

Call unto me, and I will answer thee, and shew thee great
and mighty things, which thou knowest not.

Jeremiah 33:3.

Time and again Anita and I called unto God—sometimes
together, sometimes separately. This year has tested us to our
limits at times.

But those "great and mighty things" can show up in no
other way. At times God has to stretch us out on the mat so
we dare not make a move without Him. *Then* He can deal
in a great and mighty way with the puny little life we yield
up to Him.

Fishers of Men Opportunities, Inc. was to become one of
my testing grounds wherein we all could learn just how sold
out to Jesus I intended to be.

When it turned out we had to get a license, that was okay.
But then the great search was on—including months of at-
tempting to prove to the satisfaction of state officials our
legitimate aims and purposes.

It grew a bit tedious, especially when I had to compile a diary of every transaction I had completed over a period of three years.

That chore, which nobody could do but me, nearly blew my mind. But we prayed and I persevered, and eventually I got it done. Meanwhile, Satan besieged me with doubts and discouragements on a fairly regular basis.

"What if I don't get the license?" I asked Charlie Morgan, who is a top-flight lawyer besides someone who prayed every step of the way about the future of Fishers of Men.

"The Lord is on your side," Charlie would say.

I believed it. Meanwhile, of course, we went right on with the new office—keeping things in a holding pattern of sorts —with mail stacking up and my nerves getting more and more jittery.

Teddy Heard and Anita always had given me the most beautiful encouragement where Fishers of Men was concerned. Anita and Teddy had a vision of what it would become—the top talent in America, the best Christian spokesmen, making themselves available through us to serve Jesus Christ. They both prayed about it all the time.

I missed Teddy's enthusiasm. My own was beginning to stretch pretty thin at times as the months stretched out in a series of interminable meetings and hearings, each inconclusive.

Anita had gotten about as uptight as I had before the whole thing was settled. She can be a worrywart at times, and I think toward the end she really feared Fishers of Men might fall through. She really wanted the Lord to give us a go-ahead—a clear track.

Finally we had one more hurdle to clear. Charlie Morgan and I were to appear before a state board on a Monday morning to make oral statements as to the validity of my project, and to answer questions. Charlie had written a letter which stated all pertinent facts regarding the agency.

Beyond that, we had put on the whole armor of God. All our Christian friends were praying like mad. We'd had several in for dinner on Saturday evening, Anita and I, and the whole thing ended up in a tremendous prayer session—Jody Dunton, Charlie and Marabel, Brother Bill and Peggy, all joining hands and praying their hearts out for Fishers of Men.

Another time, the Reverend John Huffman said the sweetest prayer for us. "You are well aware of Bob's need for Your helping in this calling he has from You," he began.

You know the frustrations he has faced in the last few days as his license has been blocked. You know that if he is to carry out this vision, he has to be licensed.

We thank You for the fact that You have provided office space and a high degree of interest in his project. At the same time, we ask that You will see that every detail fits into place as this week he has his final confrontation on his license. If, by any chance, this is not Your vision but only his, put all kinds of obstacles in his path. But if it's Yours, remove those troublesome aspects that could block Your plan.

And Lord, You're aware of the trauma of these past few weeks and the sudden homegoing of Teddy. We just can't understand it. It seems so premature, so unfair for her to be taken at the prime of life and ministry.

Yet thank You for the way You've given to Bob and Anita the conviction that, even through her death, a greater story can be told of Your grace and love.

Thank You that both Anita and Bob were able to stand by

her family in this time of crisis. Thank You so much for the simple, childlike trust they are displaying in Your care and your Provision.

"We thank You for the peace of God which does pass all understanding, which does keep heart, mind, and body through Christ Jesus our Lord. In His Name we pray. *Amen.*

Outside the state office building that busy Monday morning, Charlie Morgan and I prayed one more time for Fishers of Men, Inc. This would be it. We entered the meeting satisfied we had done all we could. We felt peace in our hearts, and a certainty that the Lord's will would be done. Whatever happened, we could accept it.

The rest sounds anticlimactic. We got the license. It was all very smooth and ordinary, no sweat, everything easy as can be.

Afterwards I rushed home to tell Anita, and *then* we heard some noise. She can be pretty demonstrative. We heard a few whoops of joy at that point!

Why the long, nerve-bending delay? Charlie and I believe God wanted me to see just how far I was willing to go on the side of obedience and Christian maturity.

I could have been tempted to chuck the whole thing when the going got sticky. It would have been easy to get overly discouraged as one month stretched into the next without any decision being made.

But by somehow walking with the Lord every step of the way, by determining to take the whole thing to its logical conclusion—no matter what the outcome—God showed me something very valuable.

Someone said God never starts something without intending to finish it. (*See* Philippians 1:6.) Can we say the same thing about ourselves? Do we quit too soon? As Christians, does God expect us to walk with Him to the very end of whatever project He has begun?

I believe it. I pray He helps me remember that.

In looking back, and while proofreading this book, something has occurred to me in retrospect: that we as Christians often get hung up on seeking too much advice from other well-meaning Christians regarding our problems. These well-meaning friends are often hung up themselves with their own difficulties. As I look back at all this—at all the advice we sought from our friends—I wondered that we did not go to our pastor as often as we should have. I wonder if we don't have a scriptural obligation to seek the counsel of the pastor of our home church? Our pastor should also be our friend— a family should build up a trust and rapport with him in a very personal way. If we *had* consulted more with our pastor, maybe we could have avoided some of our trials and tribulations.

The moment that license was granted, great and mighty things began to happen. We took off like a great speckled bird.

One tremendous occurrence was when Alvin Dark, one of our most appealing Christian speakers, suddenly was hired to manage the pennant-winning Oakland Athletics after being out of work for two and one-half years.

Alvin and his wife, Jackie, true born-again believers, trusted Jesus all those months while they waited for God to open a door for Alvin—who for twenty-five years had been one of the great and colorful baseball players and managers.

The story hit all the newspapers—how the Dark family hung in there with the Bible for guidance—how Jackie helped Alvin claim Deuteronomy 31:6 when things got discouraging.

Their testimony is too long to tell here, but the Darks' exciting encounters with Jesus Christ are part of the witness they give through Fishers of Men Opportunities, Inc. Anita and I were thrilled to see God open a wonderful door for Alvin.

Another exciting personality we represent is Skeeter Davis, the Country-and-Western star, whose secretary read about Fishers of Men in one of our other books and urged Skeeter to contact us.

Her Christian testimony also is dramatic. For one thing, Skeeter several months ago was suspended from the Grand Old Opry after a fifteen-year association with the show. Her offense? She spoke out in behalf of some Jesus people who frequented a Nashville shopping center.

Whatever the merits of the case, the headlines which resulted caused a number of Skeeter's bookings to cancel. All this happened at Christmas time—a particularly hard time to put your musicians out of work.

The Lord continued to try Skeeter's faith. Opportunities for work dried up; problems presented themselves on every hand. Suddenly, however, things started turning around for her. Amazing new opportunities to work, to sing, to witness, began to pop up like mushrooms. Skeeter Davis is on her way —this time in somewhat new directions as she seeks God's will for her every move.

Fishers of Men proudly offers her dedication and her talent to the glory of God. We praise God for leading Skeeter to us.

Another triumph for our organization concerns an amazing young man named David Eaton. David doesn't sing or dance or play the guitar; he's an organization man, a thoroughgoing business type with an impeccable management background.

We think the Lord outdid Himself when He led David to Fishers of Men.

One Sunday a few weeks ago this young man came forward in our church and asked the Lord to provide him with a job. Amazing, but true. A former stockbroker whose talents took him to the top very early, David Eaton got used to the good life in New York City's financial world. He was very successful and very young, and he did everything right.

David and his wife, Janet, are born-again Christians. So when their luck starting sliding (David lost his fabulous job as did many others in his field because of the nation's lack of confidence and its effect on Wall Street), they assumed the Lord would provide right away.

Thus began tedious months of job-hunting and disillusionment. Nothing worked. It was a time of intense spiritual chastening for David. He could find *nothing* to do, usually because of being "overqualified." Their situation grew desperate as the months stretched out and the money became short.

Then Janet bought one of our books—*Bless This House*—and the Eatons felt led to move to Miami Beach, and to join Northwest Baptist Church. Almost immediately David received a job offer here. All signals seemed go, so they moved down here—only to have the promised job fall through.

Then their faith took over. Broke, jobless, without prospects or any tangible hope, David and Janet have learned to

trust Jesus and to claim His promises as they never dreamed
they could or would.

Hanging on by blind faith, his pride pretty well shoved
aside now, David stepped forward to ask the church to pray
about the Lord's will for his life.

That's how we got together. Presently David Eaton—a
really fantastic business talent—is working for peanuts, helping to manage the new Fishers of Men Opportunities, Inc.
office.

It's really amazing how the Lord brought us our two fine
Christian secretaries, Judy Higgins and Diane Callicutt.
They have truly been a blessing to us personally and have
helped out so many times in so many ways in our family life.
Anita and I had been praying that a secretary would walk
in the door, because how do you go about advertising for a
Christian secretary? Then one day, Judy's mother (who is a
legal secretary in our office building) just dropped in to meet
us. She told us that their family was in the gospel music
business and that her daughter was a secretary. I asked Judy
to come in for an interview that very day, and she started
working for us the next!

How the Lord led Diane Callicutt to Fishers of Men is
even more astounding. Diane is a professional singer from
North Carolina and had been doing TV and nightclubs there.
But she wasn't happy with this kind of life. She read her
Bible, prayed, and was led to come to the Miami area. A
minister friend urged her to get in touch with me and she
shared how difficult it was to find the kind of people she
wanted to work with in the music field. I wanted Anita to
meet her and they met before the "Mike Douglas Show."
Anita invited Diane to Northwest Baptist Church that night.
Diane said later she didn't want to "force herself on the

Greens" but that Brother Bill's sermon made her feel that she should talk to Anita. Diane had mixed feelings about leaving North Carolina. Anita prayed with her that the Lord would reveal what her role should be. Our Fishers of Men license had not come through yet but when it did, we got in touch with Diane who was back home. Now she is David Eaton's assistant and will probably be doing some singing with Fishers of Men eventually.

So David, Judy, Diane, and Fishers of Men are making new starts for the Lord. Where will He have us go?

We don't know. We continue to pray. Perhaps Fishers of Men will launch David into the exact position God wants him to assume. Or maybe God intended David for us, all the time.

We think it's exciting. We're humble when the Almighty God shows His greatness to us.

Praise His Name!

# 15

# Have Thine Own Way, Lord

Teddy suffered much before she went to be with Jesus. So precariously balanced was her grip on life that she could not have medication to ease her pain.

One day, in great suffering, Teddy asked for the only sedative available to her.

"Please read the eighth chapter of Romans to me, Mama," she whispered.

Teddy gained some measure of victory over pain as she heard those God-inspired passages. Never again will I read that chapter in God's Word without recalling the faith and courage of one of God's saints.

Like Teddy, I had to learn some lessons—experience some victories—that only pain can produce. Her suffering wasted Teddy's healthy young body, a circumstance very hard for some of us to understand.

My own pain was something I found equally hard to understand, for it attacked the area of my emotions.

Now for a dogmatic Christian like me, the idea of emotional disturbance, illness, even temporary imbalance, was something I considered sin. I attributed any kind of emo-
146

tional problem to a faulty prayer life, being out of God's will, or such.

I still say God not only is the Great Physician, but the Divine Psychiatrist as well. The Christian life leads to health and stable living. Most of us can attest to that from our experiences with Christ.

Nevertheless, so many things in our lives definitely were pointing Bob and me toward serious emotional problems— factors over which we often had little or no control. We should have realized what was happening, yet we didn't.

Hardly did one severe stress situation die down before another seemed to arise, for example. And then there was the excessive fatigue we'd learned to live with; not just the body, but mind and emotions as well.

Sure we had grief, sadness, anxiety—a year of emotional seesawing.

Still, if I had to choose the very worst factor of all, I'd probably say loneliness. Bob and I had fallen into a pattern of enduring our little miseries silently, to a great extent. We did not communicate well. We didn't try to bear one another's burdens.

I'm a complex person, so maybe it's no wonder I was slow to see that this time it wasn't just a bad mood that was hard to shake—but a full-fledged snarl of grief, guilt, despair, feelings of sin and failure.

I moved into a deep depression—one which became increasingly more profound, one my prayers could not dispel. My wretchedness seemed to grow worse by the hour. I did not know what to do about it, so merely continued to try to hide the situation from others.

That can't be done, of course. Eventually I collapsed before Bob, ending up in a hysterical, sobbing heap. I could not identify my fears, could not tell him what was wrong, nor could I do anything at all for myself.

"I'm losing my mind," I wept.

"No, you're not. You're emotionally exhausted, but there's nothing wrong with your mind," Bob replied. He had put me to bed, telephoned our doctor, and now was offering me warm milk. He showed great concern and compassion, and this alarmed me almost as much as my outburst did!

I didn't know what to do. I simply wanted to return to the way we were—Bob selfishly jogging away and ignoring the kids and me, me trying to keep everything going. . . .

But no, it wouldn't work. I couldn't cope anymore; somehow I knew I could not do *one more thing*. I was a failure . . . just couldn't pretend any longer to succeed as Bob's wife —or a thousand other things . . . had to face facts, that I couldn't do it all anymore, couldn't do *anything* . . . that surely Bob must hate me. . . .

"No, I don't," he said kindly. "I love everything about you. I love you just the way you are . . . everything . . . and always have, always will.

"You're not a failure at all. You're just not able to cope any longer, and we're going to get you some help."

Then Bob told me he had managed to get reservations at the famous psychological clinic in Southern California, run by Dr. Clyde Narramore.

Dr. Narramore had lectured at our church on occasion. He is a Christian psychologist and his clinical psychologists are Christians as well. Charlie Morgan and Wyatt Heard are board members of his clinic near Los Angeles. Teddy and Wyatt decided to receive some counseling, at one time, and later told us they'd advise any happily married couple to enter into professional counseling so as to improve a good marriage even further.

So I knew about the Narramore Christian Foundation, but I wasn't about to go there. "I can't! Please, I can't. Bob, don't let me fail Jesus that way. What kind of witness would that be? What if people found out?"

"It's okay, Anita. You mustn't be ashamed. If you had appendicitis, you'd see a doctor. If your body is sick in any way, you see a doctor, and don't talk about failing Jesus.

"Baby, this time your emotions need healing. You've been through too much. We're going to help Jesus make you well, and we're on our way out to California this very afternoon."

He absolutely meant it. Within two hours Bob had packed us and gotten us to the airport. He had phoned a few friends and Brother Bill, and we were on our way. I was far from reconciled.

"I can't break down this way, Bob. How about the revival? How can I back out of singing on opening night? And how about Governor Askew? He's coming to Northwest Baptist Sunday!"

In vain did I try to change Bob's mind. Thoroughly frightened by my exhausted state, he was taking me toward the best treatment he knew how to find.

The results were dramatic. Within twenty-four hours of our arrival at the Narramore Christian Foundation I was functioning reasonably well, and knew how lucky I was to be gaining fascinating new insights into myself and my life, through Dr. Wayne Colwell's skillful therapy.

God had begun a very important work in the life of a complicated gal. I had come to understand that basically I am healthy, and through faith can claim every good and perfect gift God has to offer. I understood that.

What I never had realized in the past, though, is that God expects us to offer Him some intelligent cooperation in the business of reconditioning those unsatisfactory areas of our lives we usually designate as "hang-ups." Childhood conditioning never will be perfect. Eventually each of us must wrestle with problems of reconstructing weak or damaged areas of our lives which result from faulty pasts.

Within three days I had attained a constructive approach to my problems. Through prayer, thinking, questioning, probing, we had begun to shed great floods of light over some of the "dark rooms" in my life.

I had straightened out the nonsense about ruining my witness. In fact, by now I had begun to praise God without ceasing for the wonderful opportunity to begin making real sense out of my adult life. Fantastic!

The second night I was there, I woke up in the middle of the night and tiptoed to the bathroom. I spent most of the remainder of the night filling page after page in my notebook, explaining some of my own feelings toward certain people and on other important matters.

When I presented Wayne with *seventeen pages* of notes the next day, he whistled. "The Lord helped you," he told me. "This is a wonderful breakthrough. I'm proud of you."

Bob and I spent three days in California. I was tired and weak when we flew home late that week, but grateful to God for new insights and new strengths. He had shown me so much.

Our return to Miami Beach was so speedy I could sing at our church's revival and hear one of my favorite preachers,

Dr. J. Harold Smith. Furthermore, our governor's visit to Northwest Baptist Church with us could proceed as planned. Isn't God good!

I still had a hang-up about telling anyone I had been to the Narramore Foundation, feeling it would jeopardize my witness. "Please don't tell anyone, Bob," I begged, and he'd say, "Why should I?" I was ashamed to tell my secret to anyone at all. I felt I had compromised my witness.

Why, then, did I waste no time whatever in blurting out to Governor Reubin Askew exactly why I had gone to California, and what had been accomplished there? To my surprise, he reacted warmly.

"Anita," he said, "at some time in all our lives we go through some kind of difficult stress and pressure of varying degrees, and the first state of release is to take it to the Lord, and then by all means seek professional help, if needed. Understand yourself, and you'll find you possess the keys of the Kingdom. Above all this, Anita, I think it's very important that when the time is right, you *must* share this with your readers. My wife, Donna Lou, and I love your books and know how they have served as an inspiration to others. The biggest problem is that too many Christians are *not* willing to share the difficult part of their lives—which is just as important as sharing the testimony of their initial Christian rebirth."

And while riding in the car to our church, he shared two of his favorite poems which he said have helped him to reshape his prayer life and to help him over the times of stress and pressure. Here are the two poems that mean so much to Governor Askew, and I think you will agree that they are meaningful to all Christians:

## The Secret

I met God in the morning
　When my day was at its best,
And His presence came like sunrise,
　Like a glory in my breast.

All day long the Presence lingered,
　All day long He stayed with me,
And we sailed in perfect calmness
　O'er a very troubled sea.

Other ships were blown and battered,
　Other ships were sore distressed,
But the winds that seemed to drive them
　Brought to us a peace and rest.

Then I thought of other mornings,
　With a keen remorse of mind,
When I too had loosed the moorings,
　With the Presence left behind.

So I think I know the secret,
　Learned from many a troubled way:
You must seek Him in the morning
　If you want Him through the day!

RALPH SPAULDING CUSHMAN

## Being Still

How difficult to be "Still."
'Tis easier far to be busy than to be quiet,
To keep running harried, hectic missions
Or find some frail excuse to spin my rotors in the air

and not come down;
But I must alight,
Turn off the rotors and be still,
So He who made this frail machine
Can check and clean and oil its parts.
Give instructions for my mission,
And pump in power to
Lift me up again!

CAROLYN RHEA

The governor gave a very sweet and tender prayer in church that day and I *especially* thank God for sending such a dedicated, sensitive, loving Christian to encourage me to share with others the most difficult time of my life.

The straightening-out process within me came not a day too soon. Bob and I communicated better now. His love and patience toward me touched my heart. Obviously he rejoiced at my progress.

Then came a series of deaths, each of which produced a degree of depression. Would I be catapulted right back to my semihelpless state? I still seemed to get unnerved very easily. Bob and I, and others, were praying for a healing, knowing God desired it for me.

Dan Topping, Charlotte's husband, died at the Miami Heart Institute. The night he passed away we had just packed for a long trip to Spokane, Washington, to tape an Oral Roberts TV Special at Expo '74. I rushed over to be with Charlotte and stayed till midnight, comforting and praying with her. But when she told me, with tears in her eyes, how Dan loved me and loved to hear me sing, I knew what was coming. . . .

"Charlotte, of course I'll sing. I'd love to. But there's no way humanly possible for us to make it back in time," I told her gently. Then, boldly, I said, "But Charlotte, if God wants me to sing at Dan's funeral, He'll perform a miracle!"

She smiled and said, "You're right, Anita."

God performed *many* miracles in Spokane, and with the help and prayers of producer Dick Ross, Oral and Evelyn Roberts, Richard and Patty Roberts, Roy Clark of the "Hee Haw" Show, our own Kathie Epstein, and the rest of the World Action Singers, and all the crew, not only was the weather perfect for our outdoor taping, but we made the only plane to Miami with time to spare to change clothes and call Charlotte not to worry—that God had planned all along for me to sing at Dan's coronation!

Charlotte took Dan's death like a trooper. Dan had been baptized soon after Charlotte, Brother Bill, and I led him to the Lord. He was, to some extent, my babe in Christ—and I wept for him. At his funeral services, however, with no tears, I gave this testimony. I said exactly what God had placed on my heart:

"The world saw Dan Topping as a great man, but the greatness I saw in Dan was the day he humbled himself before a great God and, praying on his knees, asked Jesus Christ to come into his heart and become Lord of his life. The Bible says, 'What shall it profit a man if he shall gain the whole world, and lose his own soul? . . . For by grace are ye saved through faith; and that not of yourselves: it is the gift of God: Not of works, lest any man should boast'!" (I had quoted Mark 8:36 and Ephesians 2:8, 9.) Then, with Jimmy Hubbard (our secretary Judy Higgins' stepfather) accompanying on the organ, I sang all *three* stanzas of "How Great Thou Art."

Next a call came from Esther Orr, mother of Metro Miami

Mayor Jack Orr who was dying of cancer. "Would you please come over. I am praying for a miracle!"

I had visited with the mayor, his mother and family, a few weeks earlier in his apartment and had heard him testify to his faith and trust in Jesus Christ—starting from atheist to alcoholic to believer. It was quite a story to hear but I, along with others, had judged him otherwise because of some emotional hang-ups in his life. Because of my experience with Teddy's death, I was able to share with Mrs. Orr in love that God heals in two ways: He could completely heal Mayor Orr's cancer and make him well, or the greatest healing of all—He could take him home. We prayed over the phone, and I did pray for God to heal Jack Orr in "His" perfect way! As I later related to Mayor Orr's and Charlotte Topping's good friend, Brother Bud Colton (a deacon of All Souls Episcopal Church), "Esther Orr, who had been saved a few years earlier at a Billy Graham Crusade, had asked God for a miracle and God answered!" Sharing my own recent experience and using Teddy's trinity, the mayor's daughter and sister received God's greatest miracle that day—salvation! A few days later God healed Metro Miami Mayor Jack Orr— He took him to His heavenly home.

A few weeks later, Grandpa Berry passed away in Oklahoma in the nursing home where he spent his last days. When Patsy Crittenden called to tell me Grandpa had passed away, she said, "Anita, I have some wonderful news. Grandpa's with Jesus." I praised God that he was suffering and lonely no more, but I wept buckets of tears. It was similar to when Grandma Berry went to be with the Lord: I felt inconsolable.

Soon I was on my way to Oklahoma, and I knew Bob was

very concerned about me. Aunt Goldmae and Uncle Ernest Fleming picked me up in Dallas, Texas. I spent the night with them in Bridgeport going to church, visiting, and eating good home-cooked food the neighbors and ladies of their Church of Christ had brought over. Early the next morning their youngest son, my cousin John Paul Fleming, drove us to that long-familiar First Baptist Church in Tishomingo, Oklahoma, where I joined numerous other family members in paying tribute to Grandpa Berry, a man almost universally liked and admired.

Again, they wanted me to sing at the funeral. Despite the strain on myself, I yearned to please Grandpa. I *had* to sing —and again, chose "How Great Thou Art" and "Open My Eyes That I May See." I believe Grandpa would have liked that. This second song was to me a description of Grandpa's testimony for Jesus. (Before he was saved as a young man, an oil-refinery explosion had literally seared out his eyesight, but in the hospital a Baptist minister—with the influence of his own sweet Christian wife, Gracia Isola Berry—led Grandpa Berry to receive Jesus Christ as his Lord and Saviour. From then on there was no stopping John Berry from asking even perfect strangers if they were saved and sharing how he had to get his eyes put out before he could really *see!*)

And then, surveying his coffin, I did something I've never done before or since—I *totally* broke down, and in public at that.

No member of my family had seen me lose my composure before. Now I sobbed as though my heart would break. I had no idea what they thought of me, nor did I particularly care at that moment. Uncle Luther consoled me, told me it was good to let it all out, that it would be a release for me. I marveled later as to the strength and love he showed when conducting the graveside ceremony for Grandpa.

Later on, one of my cousins sought me out, wishing to console me. We fell into a sharing session. When I told her about receiving psychological treatment in recent weeks, she became almost envious.

"I know I need help," she whispered. I could see it changed her whole outlook on herself, sharing my experiences on this particular subject.

"Lord, are You trying to give me a new harvest field?" I wondered. "Perhaps there's a special ministry to people who are in pain or hurt emotionally. After all, how can any of us get through this life without finding ourselves at a disadvantage at least some of the time? Aren't we all emotionally damaged to some extent? How can I help others who have experienced the panic, grief, lethargy, and hopelessness I have known? How would You have me learn to relate to them, to share what You have done for me?"

A few days after arriving in Oklahoma Bob sent me this letter:

Anita, you have just taken off. I stood here in the office with Judy and Diane, all praying and crying for you. Come home safely to us all. Isaiah 12:2; 1 Corinthians 13:12.

And he shared this from his daily devotional:

> Light after darkness,
> Gain after loss—
> Strength after weakness,
> Crown after cross—
> Sweet after bitter,

Hope after fear—
Home after wandering,
Praise after tears—
Sheaves after sowing,
Sun after rain—
Sight after mystery,
Peace after pain—
Joy after sorrow,
Calm after blast.
Rest after *weariness,*
Sweet rest at last—
Near after distance,
Gleam after gloom—
Love after loneliness,
Life after tomb—
After long agonies,
Rapture of bliss—
Right is the pathway,
Leading to this.

Today, as the Lord helps me strengthen, Bob and I ponder the uses of suffering and pain. We have learned some things about suffering during these months; we have learned to care, and to endure, and to grow beyond the point of worst impact.

We have gained sufficient perspective now to begin to guess at God's uses of adversity in our lives. We know He utilizes every experience of our lives toward His best and most holy good.

I think of the old hymn by Adelaide A. Pollard:

Have Thine own way, Lord, Have Thine own Way!
Thou art the Potter, I am the clay.

Mold me and make me, After Thy will,
While I am waiting, yielded and still.

I *am* the clay, I think. The old vessel has been broken on the wheel; today God is shaping something newer, more useful. I do not complain about the process, but merely thank God He sees fit to reshape His vessel.

Like Teddy, I can turn to the eighth chapter of Romans for God's own comfort. "And we know that all things work together for good to them that love God, to them who are the called according to his purpose," I read in verse 28.

I think about those who are called. I think about the omnipotent and omnipatient God, who through the ages loves each of His children with the steady, burning love of a candle flame.

"Thank You that You lit my candle, Lord, that flame which will burn throughout eternity!"

Again I return to that noblest book in Romans. "Who shall separate us from the love of Christ?" I read, in that ringing passage beginning with verse 35.

And then (verse 38, 39) comes God's triumphant answer:

For I am persuaded, that neither death, nor life, nor angels, nor principalities, nor powers, nor things present, nor things to come,

Nor height, nor depth, nor any other creature, shall be able to separate us from the love of God, which is in Christ Jesus our Lord.

*Amen!*